Science
Yellow Pages
for Students and Teachers
Revised Edition

from the Kids' Stuff™ People

Incentive Publications, Inc.
Nashville, Tennessee

Special acknowledgement is accorded to

- *Marjorie Frank for compiling and organizing the materials included in this publication*
- *Susan Eaddy for the cover art*
- *Marta Drayton, Illustrator*
- *Jean K. Signor, Editor*

ISBN 0-86530-558-7
Library of Congress Control Number: 2001094394

PRINTED IN THE UNITED STATES OF AMERICA
www.incentivepublications.com

Table of Contents

Physical Science

Earth & Space Science

Life Science

SCIENCE SKILLS CHECKLIST

GENERAL SCIENCE SKILLS

Nature & History of Science

_____ Define science
_____ Show understanding of the nature of scientific research and discoveries
_____ Show understanding of science as a human endeavor
_____ Distinguish among different branches of science
_____ Show understanding of the limitations of science
_____ Identify the topics and areas associated with different branches of science
_____ Identify pursuits and studies associated with different kinds of scientists
_____ Identify some uses of science and technology
_____ Identify discoveries and areas of research associated with specific scientists in history
_____ Identify some aspects of the history of science
_____ Show understanding of the relationship between science and technology
_____ Show understanding of the relationship between natural disasters and science
_____ Show understanding of benefits and consequences to society of science and technology
_____ Show understanding of the nature and method of scientific inquiry

Science Concepts & Processes

_____ Show understanding of the concepts of change and constancy
_____ Show understanding of the concept of cycle
_____ Show understanding of the concept of cause and effect
_____ Show understanding of the concept of systems
_____ Show understanding of how a change in one component changes the system
_____ Show understanding of the concepts of order and organization
_____ Show understanding of the concept of equilibrium
_____ Show understanding of the concept of evolution
_____ Show understanding of the concept of form and function
_____ Understand and use the process of observation
_____ Understand and use the process of forming a hypothesis
_____ Understand and use the process of classification
_____ Understand and use the process of measurement
_____ Understand the process of using numbers
_____ Understand and use the processes of identifying and controlling variables
_____ Understand and use the process of interpreting data
_____ Understand and use the process of predicting
_____ Understand and use the process of designing an experiment
_____ Understand the process of using models
_____ Define terms related to science processes
_____ Understand and distinguish between characteristics of scientific laws and theories
_____ Understand the process of conducting an experiment
_____ Recognize some safety procedures for science experimentation

PHYSICAL SCIENCE SKILLS

Matter

_____ Identify characteristics of the states of matter; understand the kinetic theory of matter
_____ Recognize the effects of temperature and pressure on matter
_____ Show understanding of the concept of buoyancy
_____ Distinguish among solutions, mixtures, colloids, suspensions, homogeneous and heterogeneous mixtures
_____ Distinguish between physical and chemical properties of a substance
_____ Show understanding of the structure, components, and functions of the parts of the atom
_____ Recognize the symbols for common elements
_____ Identify features of an element from the periodic table; understand the different groupings
_____ Identify some characteristics of elements; distinguish between an element and compounds
_____ Recognize organic compounds and hydrocarbons
_____ Identify common compounds from their formulas; write formulas for common compounds
_____ Distinguish between physical and chemical changes in a substance
_____ Identify the physical changes of freezing, melting, evaporation, condensation; recognize freezing point, melting point, boiling point
_____ Show understanding of processes and components in solutions
_____ Identify solute, solvent, aqueous solutions, saturated, supersaturated; electrolyte
_____ Show understanding of how solubility of a substance can be increased
_____ Demonstrate how a formula can be used to show the chemical reaction between two substances
_____ Distinguish between balanced and unbalanced chemical equations
_____ Show understanding of the characteristics and behavior of acids and bases

Energy, Force, & Motion

_____ Define and apply concepts of force & motion (such as speed, resistance, velocity, relative velocity, acceleration, terminal velocity, freefall, momentum, inertia, etc.)
_____ Understand and calculate speed and velocity
_____ Recognize details and applications of the laws of motion
_____ Define and distinguish between potential energy and kinetic energy
_____ Understand the concept of energy transfer
_____ Recognize and apply concepts of thermal energy, heat, and heat transfer
_____ Identify scientific units used to measure energy, force, work, power, and electric current
_____ Determine amount of energy needed for heating task
_____ Describe the Law of Conservation of Energy
_____ Define and distinguish among different kinds of energy
_____ Define terms and processes related to work to identify different simple machines
_____ Define power, calculate mechanical advantage, work, and power
_____ Define concepts, processes, and terms related to electricity and magnetism and their uses
_____ Show understanding of workings of circuits
_____ Explain nuclear fusion and nuclear fission

Waves, Sound, & Light

_____ Recognize features of waves
_____ Show familiarity with the location of waves on the electromagnetic spectrum
_____ Show understanding of frequency and its relationship to wavelength
_____ Use velocity to calculate distance of sound sources
_____ Recognize the relationship between temperature and sound transfer
_____ Show understanding of materials that conduct sound
_____ Recognize relationship between amplitude and intensity of sound
_____ Show understanding of the Doppler effect of sound
_____ Recognize and explain some properties of light, lenses, and color

Science Yellow Pages, Rev. Ed.

EARTH & SPACE SCIENCE SKILLS

Space

_____ Recognize features of the solar system; identify features and position of the nine planets
_____ Distinguish between different motions of planets and bodies in space
_____ Recognize features and function of the sun
_____ Recognize phases of the moon
_____ Differentiate between a solar eclipse and a lunar eclipse; explain what happens in eclipses
_____ Identify bodies and features of outer space and their behaviors
_____ Recognize some key persons, events, and missions in space exploration

Earth's Composition, Processes, & Changes

_____ Recognize and define surface features on the Earth; recognize the concept of relief
_____ Understand the use of latitude and longitude as a system for locating places on Earth's surface
_____ Recognize features of Earth's surface and interior structure
_____ Understand the rock cycle. Show understanding of the processes by which rocks are formed
_____ Identify the three main groups of rocks and how they are formed
_____ Distinguish between igneous, metamorphic, and sedimentary rocks; identify specific rocks
_____ Use understanding of mineral characteristics and classification to identify specific minerals
_____ Distinguish between internal and external processes of change
_____ Distinguish between disintegration and decomposition as two kinds of weathering
_____ Identify ways gravity erodes the land
_____ Explain the difference between weathering and erosion
_____ Name the agents of erosion; recognize features and process of erosion by each agent
_____ Identify different kinds of volcanoes; identify features of volcanic activity
_____ Show understanding of plate tectonics and earthquake processes
_____ Identify features of earthquake activity

Earth's Waters

_____ Recognize processes by which moving water changes land
_____ Identify and define features of river systems and runoff
_____ Recognize river drainage patterns and river deposits
_____ Recognize features of lakes, swamps, and bogs
_____ Show understanding of the processes by which groundwater changes the land
_____ Show understanding of general information about Earth's lithosphere
_____ Show understanding of formation and processes of ocean currents
_____ Recognize causes and features of ocean waves
_____ Show understanding of processes that occur as waves move toward shore
_____ Distinguish between spring tides and neap tides
_____ Describe the relationship between the sun-moon-Earth system and the movement of tides
_____ Identify some features of shore zones
_____ Identify some conditions necessary for coral reef growth; distinguish among kinds of reefs
_____ Identify features of the ocean floor

Air, Climate, & Weather

_____ Identify layers of Earth's atmosphere and their features
_____ Show understanding of atmospheric pressure
_____ Discriminate among different kinds of winds and other air movements
_____ Identify different weather conditions
_____ Distinguish among different kinds of precipitation
_____ Identify different weather fronts
_____ Recognize features of different climate zones

LIFE SCIENCE SKILLS

Life Processes

_____ Identify characteristics and make-up of living things
_____ Identify examples of adaptation of living things
_____ Identify ways living organisms use energy
_____ Recognize characteristics and functions of cells; distinguish between plant and animal cells
_____ Identify components of cells and their functions
_____ Identify various cell and life processes
_____ Show understanding of the system of life classification
_____ Recognize characteristics of organisms in specific life kingdoms

Simple Organisms

_____ Identify characteristics of organisms in the moneran, protist, and fungi kingdoms
_____ Identify and recognize characteristics of monerans, viruses, bacteria, and cyanobacteria
_____ Define parasites, saprophytes, and mutualism
_____ Recognize the functions of bacteria
_____ Identify characteristics and functions of protists; distinguish among various types
_____ Describe functions of cilia, pseudopods, and flagella in protists
_____ Identify characteristics and functions of fungi; distinguish among various types
_____ Describe ways fungi can be helpful or harmful

Plants

_____ Identify characteristics of plants
_____ Identify divisions of the plant kingdom
_____ Distinguish between vascular and nonvascular plants
_____ Identify the names and functions of plant structures
_____ Show understanding of key plant processes and behaviors
_____ Show understanding of the system of plant classification
_____ Identify characteristics of different seed and seedless plants
_____ Distinguish between gymnosperms and angiosperms
_____ Identify names and functions of flower parts
_____ Show understanding of concepts related to plant reproduction, growth, and development
_____ Recognize characteristics of different kinds of soils
_____ Show understanding of the carbon dioxide-oxygen and nitrogen cycles as related to plant processes

Animals

_____ Show understanding of the system of classification of animals
_____ Recognize characteristics of organisms in the nine major animal phyla
_____ Recognize examples of organisms belonging to different animal phyla
_____ Distinguish between bilateral symmetry, radial symmetry, and no symmetry
_____ Recognize the classifications of vertebrates and invertebrates in the animal kingdom
_____ Show understanding of the numbers and complexity of animals in various phyla
_____ Recognize characteristics of different classes of animals; identify examples
_____ Identify animals in different classes of arthropods
_____ Recognize the stages in complete and incomplete metamorphosis of insects
_____ Identify characteristics of animals in the different classes of the chordate phylum
_____ Show understanding of the reproductive processes of different animal species
_____ Recognize animal behaviors; distinguish between acquired and inborn behavior
_____ Show understandings of concepts related to genetics and heredity

Science Yellow Pages, Rev. Ed.

Ecology

_____ Recognize and define different relationships within an ecosystem
_____ Distinguish between producers and consumers
_____ Distinguish between producers, and primary & secondary consumers in a food chain
_____ Recognize characteristics of different biomes
_____ Understand factors that influence the size of a population
_____ Understand the concept of succession in a community
_____ Identify fossil fuels, biodegradable substances, and nonrenewable resources
_____ Show understanding of the nitrogen, water, and carbon dioxide-oxygen cycles
_____ Describe benefits and consequences to the environment of technological choices
_____ Show understanding of effects of pollutants
_____ Recognize the value of techniques to conserve resources and protect the environment

Human Body

_____ Distinguish between cells, tissues, organs, and systems; identify different kinds of cells
_____ Identify components of and functions of different body systems
_____ Show understanding of the skeletal-muscular system; recognize different kinds of joints
_____ Identify components of the nervous system and their functions
_____ Recognize the sensory organs, their locations, and their functions
_____ Recognize organs and functions of the endocrine system
_____ Recognize structures of the circulatory system and their functions
_____ Understand the concept of blood type, donation, and receiving of blood
_____ Show understanding of the working of the heart
_____ Recognize the components of the respiratory system and their functions
_____ Show understanding of organs and function of the excretory and integumentary systems
_____ Recognize the components of the digestive system and their functions
_____ Recognize components of the reproductive system and their functions
_____ Show basic understanding of concepts related to heredity and genetics

Health & Fitness

_____ Identify some communicable diseases and their causes
_____ Show understanding of inherited diseases
_____ Recognize the function of body systems to prevent and fight disease
_____ Show understanding of the concepts of carrier, immunity, and epidemic
_____ Recognize different kinds of diseases and their symptoms
_____ Distinguish between diseases caused by viruses and those caused by bacteria
_____ Recognize different categories of diseases (congenital, degenerative, environmental, mental)
_____ Show understanding of the development and uses of vaccines
_____ Show understanding of the how the body works naturally to fight disease and infections
_____ Show understanding of some treatments used for common diseases
_____ Show understanding of ways to stop or slow the spread of disease
_____ Show understanding of uses, dangers, and body responses to drugs
_____ Show understanding of the role of the FDA in regulating food and drugs
_____ Explain the benefits of good health and fitness behaviors
_____ Show understanding of the nutrients needed by the body, their sources, and their functions
_____ Identify benefits and sources of nutrients needed by the body
_____ Identify different kinds of exercise; recognize the benefits of exercise to the body
_____ Distinguish between low-density and high-density lipoproteins
_____ Recognize body responses to stress and methods for stress management
_____ Describe appropriate responses to emergencies
_____ Show familiarity with the effects of various drug substances on the bodies and the dangers
of use or abuse of those substances.

SCIENCE CONCEPTS

When studying science, students will come in contact with some broad, underlying concepts that explain or relate to the natural and physical world. Every specific topic of study will bring students into contact with some or all of these basic concepts. An understanding of these concepts will provide students with a background against which to approach investigations about the world.

Change—Most things in the universe are in the process of changing. Change is a key part of the processes in the scientific world. Changes occur in properties, motion, positions, form, and function of objects and materials. Changes occur when materials, objects, organisms, and systems interact with each other. Changes can be described, measured, and quantified.

Constancy—While most things are changing, there are some properties and processes that remain the same. The total mass plus energy in the universe, for instance, is constant (though energy can be transferred and matter can change form).

Cycle—There are many kinds of cycles operating within the natural and physical world. Every living organism has a life cycle. There are Earth system cycles such as the tides, the movement of planets, the lives of stars, the rock cycle, the oxygen-carbon dioxide cycle, and the nitrogen cycle. Man-made systems also have cycles. Cycles exist within every field of scientific study.

Cause & Effect—Most changes, processes, and events in the universe have identifiable causes and effects. This concept is at the core of all the various science topics students will investigate. When doing investigations, students can be on the "lookout" for the causes and effects of various behaviors, interactions, actions, and changes.

Systems—A system is an organized group of related components or objects that form a whole and function as a whole. Each system has components and boundaries. Any given system is frequently related or connected to other systems. A change in one component of a system that affects the whole system. Most systems function with an input and an output of materials and energy.

Order & Organization—The behavior of objects and organisms in the universe can be described according to a certain statistical order. It is useful for students to identify and investigate the orderly behaviors and processes in the world. It is also useful to notice the types of organization in the natural and physical world. Living systems have various kinds and levels of organizations. Insight into order and organization is crucial to understanding systems.

Equilibrium—Most systems and interacting units of matter tend toward a state of balance—a steady state in which energy is uniformly distributed. Examples of the tendency toward equilibrium abound throughout all areas of scientific study.

Evolution—Things in the natural and man-made world change over time. The present forms and functions of systems, organisms, objects, and materials have arisen from the past.

Structure & Function—Form and function are complementary factors for most organisms and systems. Very often the form or structure of something affects its use or function. Understanding the relationship between the form of an object, organism, or system and its function is critical to understanding the workings of that object, organism, or system.

Energy & Matter—Energy and matter are intricately connected to one another; energy and matter are constantly interacting with and changing one another

SCIENCE METHODS & PROCESSES

Scientific Method

To uncover facts and solve mysteries, scientists use scientific methods. There are basic steps in each method; however, the steps need not be followed in any particular order. The basic components of any scientific method include the following:

• stating the problem

• gathering information

• suggesting an answer for the problem

• performing an experiment to test the answer

• recording and analyzing the results of experiments or other observations

• stating conclusions

• posing new questions raised by the conclusions

Scientific Processes

When following a scientific method, scientific process skills such as these are used:

Classifying — arranging data in a logical order

Communicating — exchanging information

Comparing — observing how things are alike or different

Controlling Variables — managing factors that may influence an experiment

Defining Operationally — listing the criteria by which something is defined

Experimenting — testing under controlled conditions

Formulating Models — devising a concrete representation to illustrate abstract relationships of objects

Hypothesizing — tentatively accepting an explanation as the basis for further investigation

Inferring — deducing a conclusion from available evidence

Interpreting Data — finding patterns or relationships in a set of data

Measuring — determining magnitude in terms of the number of units

Observing — using the senses to obtain information

Predicting — foretelling from previous information

Questioning — raising uncertainty

Recording Data — gathering and systematically storing important items of information

Relating Time and Space — describing how position changes with time

SOME BRANCHES OF SCIENCE

Aerodynamics — study of the mechanics of motion between air and a solid

Agronomy — study of soil and crop-raising

Anatomy — study of the structure of organisms

Anthropology — study of the origin and development of human cultures

Archaeology — study of remains from past cultures

Astronomy — study of the universe: stars, planets, and all heavenly bodies

Astrophysics — study of the chemical and physical nature of objects in space

Bacteriology — study of bacteria

Biochemistry — study of the chemical makeup of cells in order to determine the life processes of cells and entire organisms

Biophysics — study of the physical processes in the functioning of living things

Biology — study of the science of life processes of plants and animals

Botany — study of plants

Cartography — making of maps or charts

Chemical Engineering — application of chemistry to industrial and technological uses

Chemistry — study of the makeup and properties of substances and of their reactions to one another

Climatology — study of weather trends and patterns over a period of time

Computer Science — study and application of the science of computer programming and use

Ecology — study of the relationships between living things in the environment

Economics — study of human production, distribution, and use of goods and services

Electronics — application of the scientific technology of electricity in such ways as the design and application of circuitry and equipment for power generation, machine control, and communications

Embryology — study of fetal development

Engineering — application of the science and math which makes the properties of matter and energy useful to people through structures, machines, systems, or products

Entomology — study of insects and insect control

Environmental Science — study and application of methods to manage, protect, and repair the environment

Forestry — science of planting and managing forests

Genetics — study of heredity and genes

Geography — study of the physical structures of Earth's surface and their relationships to human life and cultures

Science Yellow Pages, Rev. Ed.

Geology — study of the structure, makeup, and history of Earth, and of Earth's changes

Histology — study of tissues

Ichthyology — study of fish

Marine Biology — study of the plants and animals that live in the ocean

Marine Geology — study of the ocean floor

Mathematics — science of logical reasoning and calculation with numbers and other ways of counting or measuring

Medicine — study, prevention, and treatment of sickness, injury, and disease

Meteorology — study of the atmosphere and the physical and chemical processes that take place in the atmosphere and produce weather

Microbiology — study of organisms that can be seen only with the aid of a microscope

Mineralogy — study of minerals

Molecular Biology — study of the structure and function of large molecules necessary to life

Nuclear Physics — study and application of physics as it deals with the structure of atomic nuclei, nuclear forces, the fission process, the study of radioactive decay, etc.

Neurology — study and treatment of the structure and diseases of the nervous system

Oceanography — study of the physical properties and processes and inhabitants of the ocean

Organic Chemistry — study of compounds containing the element carbon

Ornithology — study of birds

Paleontology — study of past geological periods as revealed through remains in rocks

Petrology — study of rocks

Physics — study of matter and energy

Physiology — study of the normal functions of living things and their parts

Political Science — study of forms of government and all other aspects of politics

Psychology — study of human mental processes and human behavior, including disorders

Radiology — science of dealing with X-rays, other forms of radiant energy, and other forms of technology for viewing bones and organs and for diagnosing and treating disease

Seismology — study of earthquakes and other earth vibrations

Sociology — study of the origin, nature, and development of human society

Taxonomy — classification of living things

Thermodynamics — study of heat as it is produced by the motion of molecules

Zoology — study of the life, structure, growth, and classification of animals

SOME MEMORABLE SCIENTISTS AND THEIR WORK

Aristotle — (300s BC) a Greek philosopher noted for his works on logic, metaphysics, ethics, and politics who was also the first to attempt a classification of animals

Amedeo Avogadro — (early 1800s) an Italian physicist who discovered the molecule. A law was named after him which states that equal volumes of gases under identical conditions of temperature and pressure contain the same number of molecules.

Alexander Graham Bell — (late 1800s–early 1900s) an American inventor who invented the telephone and who became an expert in teaching deaf people to speak

George Washington Carver — (early 1900s) an American botanist and chemist who discovered over 300 products that can be made from peanuts: such as oil, cheese, soap, and coffee

Nicolaus Copernicus — (around 1500) a Polish astronomer who waited a lifetime before publishing his conviction that the sun, not the earth, is the center of the solar system

Marie & Pierre Curie — (late 1800s–early 1900s) French scientists known for their work on radioactivity and discovery of radioactive elements

John Dalton — (late 1700s–early 1800s) an English chemist and physicist known for his atomic theory

Charles Darwin — (1800s) an English naturalist who traced the origin of man and wrote a book titled *The Origin of Species by Means of Natural Selection*

Thomas Alva Edison — (late 1800s–early 1900s) an American inventor who developed the electric light, the phonograph, the storage battery, the mimeograph machine, and motion pictures

Albert Einstein — (early 1900s) an American physicist who discovered that mass can be changed into energy and that energy can be changed into matter. He represented this discovery with the equation $E=mc^2$. He is also known for the Theory of Relativity.

Michael Faraday — (early 1800s) an English scientist who was able to change electromagnetic force into mechanical force, which led to the development of the first electric generator and electric motor

Alexander Fleming — (early 1900s) an English bacteriologist who discovered that a certain mold could destroy certain types of bacteria and who consequently developed penicillin

Henry Ford — (early 1900s) an American inventor who built the first gasoline engine and the first automobile. He also developed the first assembly line to speed up the production of automobiles.

Benjamin Franklin — (mid-late 1700s) often referred to as the Father of American Science. By experimenting with a kite, a key, and a bolt of lightning during an electrical storm, he was able to prove that lightning and electricity are the same thing.

Sigmund Freud — (late 1800s) an Austrian physician who established the field of psychoanalysis

Galileo Galilei — (early 1600s) an Italian astronomer and physicist who formulated the Law of Falling Bodies and wrote about acceleration, motion, and gravity. He also developed the first astronomical telescope and discovered the four moons of Jupiter.

William Harvey — (1600s) an English physician who showed how blood circulates through the human body

Heinrich Hertz — (late 1880s) a German physicist who discovered electromagnetic radiation

Hippocrates — (300–400 B.C.) a Greek physician who founded the first school of medicine and became known as the Father of Medicine as a result

Edward Jenner — (late 1900s) an English physician who founded the science of immunology by developing a vaccine to protect the body against smallpox

James Joule — (1840s) an English physicist who showed that heat is a form of energy

Carolus Linnaeus — (mid-1700s) a Swedish naturalist and physicist who devised a systematic method for classifying plants and animals

Gregor Johann Mendel — (mid-1800s) an Austrian monk and botanist who founded genetics through his work with recessive and dominant characteristics of plants

Dmitri Ivanovich Mendeleev — (late 1800s) a Russian chemist who developed the periodic classification of the elements in 1869

Sir Isaac Newton — (1600s) an English scientist and mathematician who discovered that the force of gravity is dependent upon the amount of matter in bodies and the distances between the bodies. He formulated the laws of gravity and motion and the elements of differential calculus.

Louis Pasteur — (mid 1800s) a French chemist and bacteriologist who developed a method for destroying disease-producing bacteria and for checking the activity of fermentative bacteria— (pasteurization). He developed an effective treatment for rabies.

Pythagoras — (500s B.C.) a Greek philosopher and mathematician who developed the Pythagorean theorem which states that the sum of the squares of the legs of a right triangle is equal to the square of the hypotenuse

Jonas Salk — (mid 1900s) an American physician and bacteriologist who developed a vaccine to prevent polio

James Watt — (late 1700s) a Scottish engineer and inventor who invented the modern steam engine. The "watt", a measure of electrical power, was named after him.

Eli Whitney — (late 1700s–early 1800s) an American inventor who invented the cotton gin and developed a faster way to make manufactured goods

Orville and Wilbur Wright — (early 1900s) American brothers who made the first controlled and sustained airplane flight at Kitty Hawk, North Carolina on December 17, 1903

LABORATORY SAFETY PROCEDURES

- Make sure that all chemicals are properly labeled and stored.
- Be sure there is easy access to fire extinguishers, first-aid kits, safety shower, fire blankets, running water, and eyewash stations from the laboratory.
- Wear proper eye protection devices when participating in or observing experiments involving potential eye hazards.
- Use heat-safety items such as safety tongs, asbestos mittens, aprons and rubber gloves.
- Confine long hair and loose clothing. Laboratory aprons should be worn at all times.
- Carefully read all labels and instructions.
- If you spill a chemical, wash it off immediately with water, and report the spill immediately.
- When heating a liquid in a test tube, hold the tube with a holder.
- When heating a solid in a test tube, place the tube in a stand and move the flame of the burner back and forth to evenly heat the contents.
- Never eat or drink in the lab or use lab containers as food or drink containers.
- Never inhale or taste any substance in the lab.
- Never point the open end of a heated test tube toward yourself or any other person.
- Work areas, including floors and counters, should be kept dry. Never handle electrical equipment with wet hands.
- If fire breaks out, smother it with a fire blanket or heavy coat, or use a safety shower. Never run!
- When cleaning up, return all materials properly, turn off all gas and water, disconnect electrical plugs, dispose of chemicals and materials properly, and wash your hands thoroughly.

PARTS OF A COMPOUND MICROSCOPE

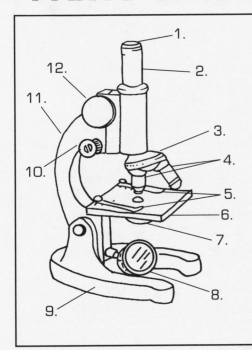

1. **Eyepiece** (contains the magnifying lens)
2. **Body tube** (separates eyepiece & lenses)
3. **Nosepiece** (holds objective lens and can be rotated to change magnification)
4. **Objective lenses** (a low-power lens {10x magnification} & a high-power lens {40x magnification})
5. **Stage clips** (hold slide in place)
6. **Stage** (table on which slide is placed)
7. **Diaphragm** (regulates the amount of light in tube)
8. **Mirror** (reflects the light upward)
9. **Base** (supports the microscope)
10. **Fine adjustment knob** (moves body tube for fine focus)
11. **Arm** (supports all components above the base)
12. **Coarse adjustment knob** (moves body tube for coarse focus)

Science Yellow Pages, Rev. Ed.

25 SIMPLE MICROSCOPE INVESTIGATIONS

1. **Yarn and thread**: Examine a variety of weights and textures of ribbon, rope, twine, yarn, and string.

2. **Mold**: Observe the structure of mold on bread or fruit. Leave the moldy food on a slide for one day. Note the changes that have occurred since the first observation.

3. **Cloth fibers**: Compare the structures of cotton, rayon, nylon, silk, and polyester.

4. **Fingerprints**: Press a finger on carbon paper or an inkpad and them on clean paper to make a print. Examine the fingerprint.

5. **Insects**: Collect a variety of dead insects and study their different structures.

6. **Onionskin**: Peel a very thin layer from the white skin of an onion. Locate cells and examine their structures.

7. **Pepper**: Note the structure of pepper. Compare the magnified pepper to salt, sugar, and any other spices.

8. **Iron filings**: Observe several iron filings. Look for ways that they vary in size and shape.

9. **Money**: Observe the different patterns and markings of various coins and bills.

10. **Hair**: Compare hairs of different people and animals. Examine samples of different colors and thickness.

11. **Chalk**: Rub a piece of chalk on sandpaper and cut a sample to make a slide. Examine the chalk dust and the sandpaper.

12. **Water**: Collect water samples after a rain from puddles, leaves, and grass. Examine a drop from each surface and compare it to a drop of tap water, soapy water, salt water, etc.

13. **Color printing**: Study different colors and patterns in colored newspaper comics.

14. **Crystals**: Compare the crystal shapes of Epsom salts, boric acid, baking soda, bicarbonate of soda, copper sulfate and other crystals.

15. **Seeds**: Collect seeds and compare their shapes, structures, and interiors.

16. **Foods**: Examine parts of fruits, vegetables, cereals, breads, and other foods.

17. **Wood shavings**: Compare wood shavings from a variety of trees.

18. **Soil**: Study the differences in samples of clay, sand, and earth.

19. **Feathers**: Find and examine feathers from different birds.

20. **Rocks**: Look for crystals of varying sizes in pieces of rock.

21. **Salt**: Look for cube-shaped crystals.

22. **Sugar**: Look for interesting crystal shapes. Place a drop of water on the slide and watch the crystals dissolve.

23. **Soap**: Examine and compare shavings from different kinds of soap.

24. **Potato starch**: Scrape a potato and study the starch granules.

25. **Printing**: Study words printed on paper, cloth, or plastic.

SOME KEY SCIENTIFIC LAWS & PRINCIPLES

Archimedes' Principle — The loss of weight of an object in water is equal to the weight of the displaced water.

Beer's Law — a law governing the absorption of light passing through a medium. No substance is perfectly transparent, but some of the light passing through the substance is always absorbed.

Beodes' Law — an empirical rule that gives the approximate relative distances of the planets from the sun

Boyle's Law — The volume of a fixed amount of gas varies inversely with the temperature of the gas, provided the pressure does not change.

Charles' Law — The volume of a fixed amount of gas varies directly with the pressure of the gas.

Law of Action — Newton's second law of motion: The acceleration of an object depends upon its mass and the applied force.

Law of Conservation of Matter — Matter is neither created nor destroyed in a chemical change, but is only rearranged.

Law of Inertia — Newton's first law of motion: A mass moving at a constant velocity tends to continue moving at that velocity unless acted upon by an outside force.

Law of Reaction — Newton's third law of motion: For every action there is an equal and opposite reaction

Law of Universal Gravitation — A gravitational force is present between any two objects. The size of the force depends on the masses of the two objects and the distance between the two objects.

Newton's Law of Gravitation — All objects exert an attractive force on one another.

Principle of Uniformitarianism — The processes that act on Earth's surface today are the same as the processes that have acted upon Earth's surface in the past.

SCIENTIFIC FORMULAS

acceleration = change in velocity/time
$$a = \Delta v/t$$

density = mass/volume
$$D = m/v$$

force = mass x acceleration
$$F = m \times a$$

momentum = mass x velocity
$$M = m \times v$$

power = work (force x distance)/time
$$P = F \times d/t$$

pressure = force/area
$$P = F/a$$

velocity (speed) = distance/time
$$v = d/t$$

volume = length x width x height
$$V = l \times w \times h$$

work = force x distance
$$W = f \times d$$

Science Yellow Pages, Rev. Ed.

TABLES OF MEASURE

LENGTH
Metric System

1 centimeter (cm) = 10 millimeters (mm)
1 decimeter (dm) = 10 centimeters (cm)
1 meter (m) = 10 decimeters (dm)
1 meter (m) = 100 centimeters (cm)
1 decameter (dkm) = 10 meters (m)
1 kilometer (km) = 1000 meters (m)

English System

1 foot (ft) = 12 inches (in)
1 yard (yd) = 36 inches (in)
1 yard (yd) = 3 feet (ft)
1 rod (rd) = 16½ feet (ft)
1 mile (mi) = 5280 feet (ft)
1 mile (mi) = 1760 yards (yd)

WEIGHT
Metric System

1 gram (g) = 1000 milligrams (mg)
1 kilogram (kg) = 1000 grams (g)
1 metric ton (t) = 1000 kilograms (kg)

English System

1 pound (lb.) = 16 ounces (oz)
1 ton (T) = 2000 pounds (lb)

CAPACITY
Metric System

1 liter (L) =1000 milliliters (mL)
1 decaliter (dkL) =10 liters (L)
1 kiloliter (kL) =1000 liters (L)

English System

1 pint (pt) = 2 cups (c)
1 quart (qt) = 2 pints (pt)
1 gallon (gal) = 4 quarts (qt)
1 peck (pk) = 8 quarts (qt)
1 bushel (bu) = 4 pecks (pk)

TEMPERATURE
Fahrenheit Scale
& Celsius (Centigrade) Scale

	Fahrenheit	Celsius
Normal body temperature:	98.6°	37°
Boiling point of water:	212°	100°
Freezing point of water:	32°	0°

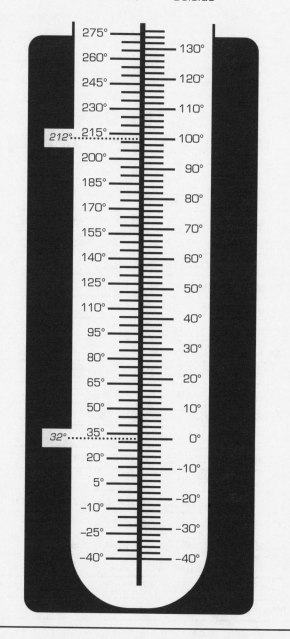

STUDENT CHECKLIST
FOR SCIENCE FAIR PROJECTS

_____ Does your project focus on a specific problem? Do you have a hypothesis?

_____ Can your question be answered through a scientific investigation?

_____ Do you have a set of expectations for this investigation?

_____ Have you stated your expectations before beginning the actual test?

_____ Do you have a materials and/or equipment list?

_____ Have you identified the variables for your investigation?

_____ Could someone else repeat your investigation from your step-by-step directions?

_____ Can your investigation be measured in specific units?

_____ Have you taken pictures, made sketches, and/or kept a log?

_____ Have you determined a table, chart, or graph form?

_____ Will your data allow you to draw conclusions and/or support your hypothesis?

_____ Do you have a plan for creatively displaying your investigation procedure and results?

TEACHER'S ASSESSMENT FOR
STUDENT SCIENCE PROJECTS & EXPERIMENTS

	Less Than Adequate	Adequate	Excellent
Shows active participation in planned activities			
Organizes equipment and materials for experimentation			
Identifies variables before beginning experimentation			
Follows a scientific method, applies scientific process skills			
Formulates a hypothesis			
Applies observation skills			
Applies classification skills			
Records data accurately			
Demonstrates scientific curiosity			
Understands use of scientific terms and symbols			
Reads, interprets, and constructs graphs and tables			
Recognizes patterns and relationships			
Predicts outcomes			
Interprets test results by synthesizing information			
Formulates reliable conclusions			
Applies problem solving techniques			
Demonstrates effective use of time			
Shows care and ability with equipment			
Follows safety precautions			
Shows care and ability in lab cleanup			

Science Yellow Pages, Rev. Ed.

PHYSICAL SCIENCE
45 STUDENT INVESTIGATIONS

1. How does sound travel?

2. What makes sounds differ?

3. How does the human ear hear sound?

4. What happens to make a thunderclap?

5. What are echoes and what causes them?

6. What kinds of materials can carry sound?

7. What is music?

8. What different kinds of waves can be found in the electromagnetic spectrum?

9. From where does light come?

10. How does light travel?

11. What is the difference between source light and reflected light?

12. How do mirrors work?

13. How does a camera work?

14. How does the human eye work?

15. What different kinds of shadows are there?

16. Why do objects have different colors?

17. How is friction overcome?

18. Why do things fall?

19. How fast do objects fall?

20. What is the difference between speed, velocity, and acceleration?

21. What causes gravity?

22. What are the various forms of energy?

23. What happens to energy after it is used?

24. How can work be measured?

25. What is density and how does one find the density of a liquid or solid?

26. What is Archimedes' Principle?

27. What is temperature and how is it measured?

28. What is magnetism?

29. How is the earth like a magnet?

30. How can magnetism be destroyed?

31. What kinds of objects do magnets attract?

32. How can one illustrate a magnetic field?

33. How can one make a homemade compass?

34. How does electricity work for people's needs?

35. What are insulators and conductors of electricity?

36. What is an electric circuit, and how is a parallel circuit different from a series circuit?

37. What is Ohm's Law?

38. How does one determine the positive pole of a battery?

39. How does a fuse work?

40. What does the periodic table show and tell about the elements?

41. Of what are atoms composed?

42. What is the difference between an element and a compound?

43. What is the difference between a mixture and a compound?

44. What are physical and chemical changes?

45. What are chemical equations?

PROPERTIES AND USES OF ACIDS & BASES

Common Acids

Name	Formula
Boric Acid	H_3BO_3
Carbonic Acid	H_2CO_3
Hydrochloric Acid	HCl
Nitric Acid	HNO_3
Phosphoric Acid	H_3PO_4
Sulfuric Acid	H_2SO_4

Properties of Acids

Neutralize bases
Turn litmus paper red
Taste sour
React with many metals to produce hydrogen
Conduct electricity

Uses of Acids

water treatment
household cleaning products
used to etch metals and glass
used in batteries
production of synthetic fibers

Common Bases

Name	Formula
Aluminum Hydroxide	$AL(OH)_3$
Ammonium Hydroxide	NH_4OH
Calcium Hydroxide	$Ca(OH)_2$
Potassium Hydroxide	KOH
Sodium Hydroxide	$NaOH$

Properties of Bases

Neutralize acids
Turn litmus paper blue
Taste bitter
Feel slippery
Conduct electricity

Uses of Bases

soap, glass
milk of magnesia
mortar
coagulants for water purification
ammonia water
lye soap

THE pH SCALE

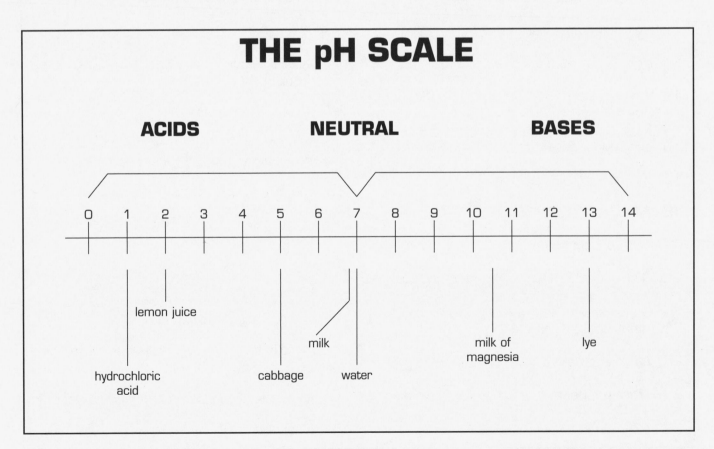

Science Yellow Pages, Rev. Ed.

CHARACTERISTICS OF SOME MIXED-UP SUBSTANCES

Characteristics of Mixtures

- A mixture is made up of two or more substances that are mixed together.
- The substances in a mixture retain their individual properties.
- The substances in a mixture can be separated by physical means.
- A mixture has no definite chemical composition.
- A mixture has no chemical formula.

Characteristics of Compounds

- A compound is made up of two or more substances which are chemically combined.
- A compound has new properties unlike those of the substances that make up the compound.
- A compound can be separated only by chemical means.
- A compound has a definite chemical composition.
- A compound has a chemical formula.

Characteristics of Solutions

- A solution is a homogeneous mixture (same in structure.)
- A solution is made of one or more liquid, gaseous, or solid substances dispersed in another.
- The particles in a solution dissolve.
- Solutes (substances that are dissolved in a solution) dissolve faster in a solution when they are stirred.
- Solutes dissolve faster in hot solutions than in cool solutions.
- Solutes dissolve faster in a solution when they are broken into small particles.
- A warm solvent (substance in which a solute dissolves) can usually hold more dissolved solute than a cold solvent.
- Saturated solutions contain all of the dissolved solute that they can hold
- Unsaturated solutions can dissolve more solute.

Characteristics of Suspensions

- A suspension is a mixture of two or more substances.
- A suspension is cloudy.
- The particles in a suspension do not dissolve.
- A suspension usually settles on standing.
- Filtering can separate a suspension.
- The particles in a suspension are larger than molecular size.

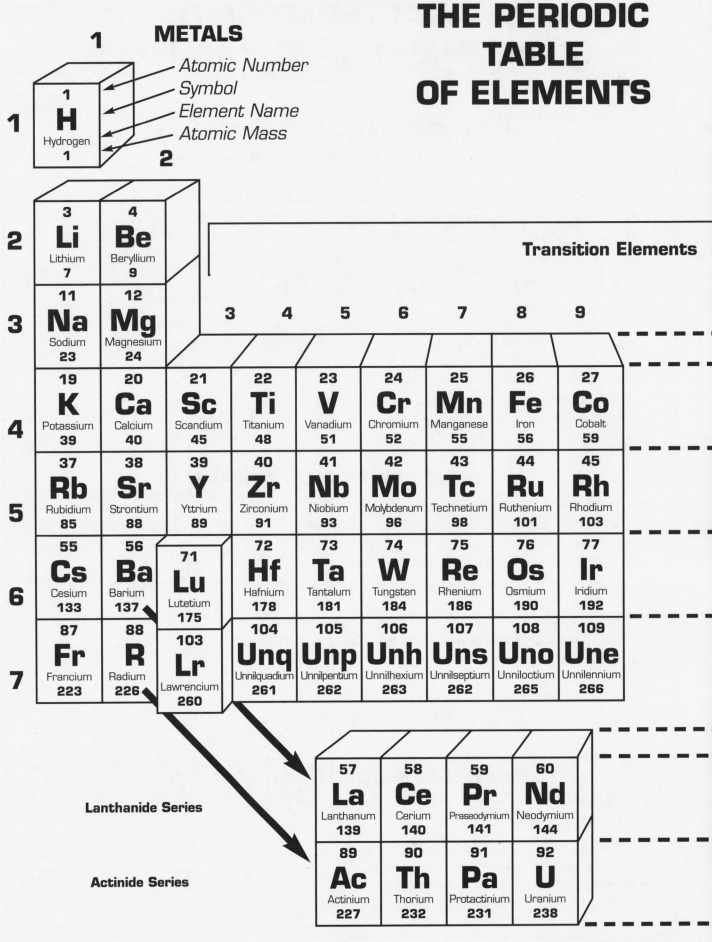

THE PERIODIC TABLE OF ELEMENTS

METALS

1

Atomic Number
Symbol
Element Name
Atomic Mass

1
H
Hydrogen
1

Transition Elements

	1	2	3	4	5	6	7	8	9
2		3 **Li** Lithium 7	4 **Be** Beryllium 9						
3	11 **Na** Sodium 23	12 **Mg** Magnesium 24							
4	19 **K** Potassium 39	20 **Ca** Calcium 40	21 **Sc** Scandium 45	22 **Ti** Titanium 48	23 **V** Vanadium 51	24 **Cr** Chromium 52	25 **Mn** Manganese 55	26 **Fe** Iron 56	27 **Co** Cobalt 59
5	37 **Rb** Rubidium 85	38 **Sr** Strontium 88	39 **Y** Yttrium 89	40 **Zr** Zirconium 91	41 **Nb** Niobium 93	42 **Mo** Molybdenum 96	43 **Tc** Technetium 98	44 **Ru** Ruthenium 101	45 **Rh** Rhodium 103
6	55 **Cs** Cesium 133	56 **Ba** Barium 137	71 **Lu** Lutetium 175	72 **Hf** Hafnium 178	73 **Ta** Tantalum 181	74 **W** Tungsten 184	75 **Re** Rhenium 186	76 **Os** Osmium 190	77 **Ir** Iridium 192
7	87 **Fr** Francium 223	88 **R** Radium 226	103 **Lr** Lawrencium 260	104 **Unq** Unnilquadium 261	105 **Unp** Unnilpentium 262	106 **Unh** Unnilhexium 263	107 **Uns** Unnilseptium 262	108 **Uno** Unniloctium 265	109 **Une** Unnilennium 266

Lanthanide Series

57 **La** Lanthanum 139	58 **Ce** Cerium 140	59 **Pr** Praseodymium 141	60 **Nd** Neodymium 144

Actinide Series

89 **Ac** Actinium 227	90 **Th** Thorium 232	91 **Pa** Protactinium 231	92 **U** Uranium 238

Science Yellow Pages, Rev. Ed.

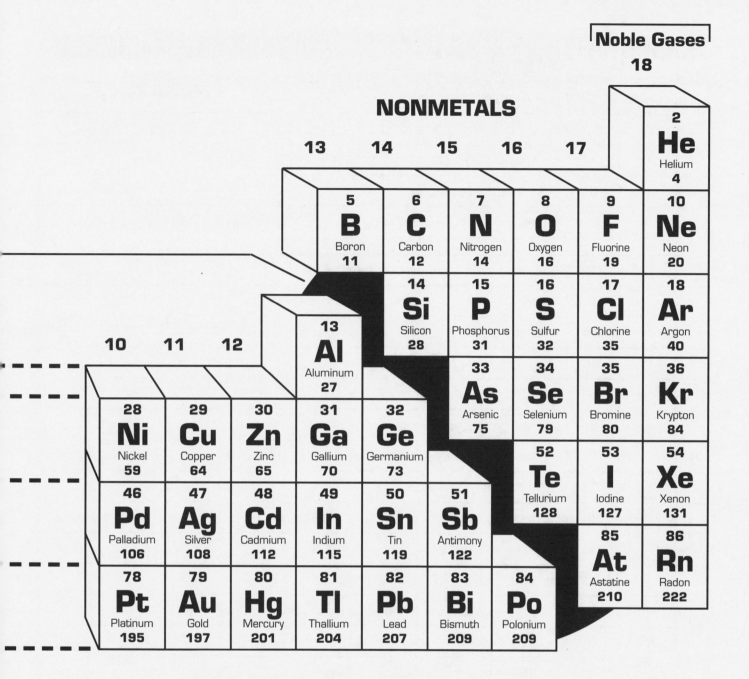

Noble Gases

NONMETALS

13	14	15	16	17	18
					2 **He** Helium 4
5 **B** Boron 11	6 **C** Carbon 12	7 **N** Nitrogen 14	8 **O** Oxygen 16	9 **F** Fluorine 19	10 **Ne** Neon 20
13 **Al** Aluminum 27	14 **Si** Silicon 28	15 **P** Phosphorus 31	16 **S** Sulfur 32	17 **Cl** Chlorine 35	18 **Ar** Argon 40

10	11	12						
28 **Ni** Nickel 59	29 **Cu** Copper 64	30 **Zn** Zinc 65	31 **Ga** Gallium 70	32 **Ge** Germanium 73	33 **As** Arsenic 75	34 **Se** Selenium 79	35 **Br** Bromine 80	36 **Kr** Krypton 84
46 **Pd** Palladium 106	47 **Ag** Silver 108	48 **Cd** Cadmium 112	49 **In** Indium 115	50 **Sn** Tin 119	51 **Sb** Antimony 122	52 **Te** Tellurium 128	53 **I** Iodine 127	54 **Xe** Xenon 131
78 **Pt** Platinum 195	79 **Au** Gold 197	80 **Hg** Mercury 201	81 **Tl** Thallium 204	82 **Pb** Lead 207	83 **Bi** Bismuth 209	84 **Po** Polonium 209	85 **At** Astatine 210	86 **Rn** Radon 222

61 **Pm** Promethium 145	62 **Sm** Samarium 150	63 **Eu** Europium 152	64 **Gd** Gadolinium 157	65 **Tb** Terbium 159	66 **Dy** Dysprosium 163	67 **Ho** Holmium 165	68 **Er** Erbium 167	69 **Tm** Thulium 169	70 **Yb** Ytterbium 173
93 **Np** Neptunium 237	94 **Pu** Plutonium 244	95 **Am** Americium 243	96 **Cm** Curium 247	97 **Bk** Berkelium 247	98 **Cf** Californium 251	99 **Es** Einsteinium 252	100 **Fm** Fermium 257	101 **Md** Mendelevium 259	102 **No** Nobelium 259

COMMON ELEMENTS AND THEIR USES

aluminum	Al	a light metal used in making airplanes, buildings, pots and pans, etc.
bromine	Br	used in photography, medicines, insecticides, etc.
calcium	Ca	a soft, metallic chemical element found in limestone, marble, chalk, etc.
carbon	C	found in coal, oil, gas, living things, and inks
chlorine	Cl	used in bleach, in chemicals to kill germs in swimming pools, and found with the element sodium in table salt
chromium	Cr	a shiny metal used on bumpers of some cars, household fixtures, etc.
copper	Cu	a metal used for electric wires, pots, pans, and pennies
gold	Au	a metal used for jewelry and precious decorative pieces
helium	He	a gas much lighter than air used in blimps and balloons
hydrogen	H	a flammable and explosive gas
iodine	I	used on cuts and wounds to kill germs
iron	Fe	a strong metal used in the construction of buildings, steel, and machines
lead	Pb	a metal used in automobile batteries and in fishing and diving weights
mercury	Hg	a heavy, poisonous liquid used in some thermometers
neon	Ne	a gas used in many lights and signs
nickel	Ni	a metal used in coins
nitrogen	N	the main gas in the air, also used in fertilizers
oxygen	O	a gas necessary for respiration; aids burning
platinum	Pt	an expensive metal used in jewelry
potassium	K	found in fertilizers
silicon	Si	used in electronics and in compounds for making glass
silver	Ag	used in tableware, jewelry, photography, medicines, and coins
sodium	Na	soft metal that combines with chlorine to make table salt
sulfur	S	used to make sulfuric acid and some medicines such as pet powders
tin	Sn	used to make cans
tungsten	W	a metal used in light bulb filaments
uranium	U	a metal used in some nuclear reactions
zinc	Zn	a metal that prevents rust and is used in dry cell batteries

Science Yellow Pages, Rev. Ed.

FLAME TESTS FOR COMMON ELEMENTS

Material to be Tested	Element Which Makes the Color	Color of the Flame
Barium nitrate	Barium (Ba)	Yellow green
Boric acid	Boron (B)	Green
Calcium chloride	Calcium (Ca)	Orange
Copper sulfate	Copper (Cu)	Bright green
Lithium nitrate	Lithium (Li)	Dark red
Potassium dichromate	Potassium (K)	Violet
Sodium chloride	Sodium (Na)	Yellow
Strontium nitrate	Strontium (Sr)	Crimson

COMMON HYDROCARBONS AND THEIR USES

Compounds that contain only hydrogen and carbon are called hydrocarbons. Hydrocarbons may be subdivided according to the types of bonds they contain. Saturated hydrocarbons (alkanes) contain only single bonds. Unsaturated hydrocarbons (alkene or alkyne) contain double or triple bonds.

Name	Chemical Formula	Use
Butane	C_4H_{10}	Used in portable lighters, home heating fuel, portable stoves and heaters
Ethane	C_2H_6	Used to make ethyl alcohol, acetic acid, and other chemicals and also used as a refrigerant
Heptane	C_7H_{16}	Often used as a main part of turpentine
Hexane	C_6H_{14}	used as a major part of certain motor fuels and dry cleaning solvents
Methane	CH_4	used as a raw material for many synthetic products and as a major part of natural gas
Octane	C_8H_{18}	used as an important part of gasoline fuel for cars, trucks, buses, etc.
Pentane	C_5H_{12}	A solvent which is commonly used as the measuring column in low-temperature thermometers
Propane	C_3H_8	Used as a "bottled gas" for home heating, portable stoves and heaters and also as a refrigerant

SIX SIMPLE MACHINES

1. Wheel and Axle — A wheel and axle consists of a small wheel (the axle) attached to the center of a large wheel. When effort is applied to the wheel, the wheel and axle spread the force over a greater distance.

2. Screw — A screw consists of a cylindrical piece of metal threaded evenly around its outside surface with an advancing spiral ridge. Screws are basically twisting inclined planes which change the direction of force. Screws may have flat or rounded heads and pointed or flat tips.

3. Wedge — A wedge is actually two inclined planes placed back to back. One end of a wedge is wide and the other end tapers to a thin edge. Wedges are used to split or cut things. *Examples: ax, snowplow, point of a nail, pin, or thumbtack*

4. Lever — A lever is a bar made of a strong material that rests on a point called a fulcrum. A lever may change the direction as well as the amount of force. The three kinds of levers are pictured below.

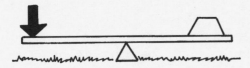

First-class lever

Second-class lever

Third-class lever

5. Pulley — A pulley is a wheel with a grooved rim, on which a rope moves or turns. By pulling one end of the rope, the wheel turns and lifts the load at the other end of the rope. A fixed pulley is attached to a support and does not move. A moveable pulley is attached to a load and moves as the load moves. *Examples: flagpoles, tow trucks*

6. Inclined Plane — An inclined plane is a flat surface set at an angle (other than a right angle) against a horizontal surface. Inclined planes change the amount of force needed to do work. The steeper the slant, the more work it takes to go up the inclined plane. *Examples: ramps*

Science Yellow Pages, Rev. Ed.

ELECTRIC CURRENT
AND THE DRY CELL BATTERY

Electric Current

Electric current is the movement of electrons through a wire.

The force used to "push" the electrons along the wire is produced by a battery and is called the electromotive force. Electromotive force is measured in volts, a unit named after Alessandro Volta, the inventor of the first battery.

How A Battery Works

A battery is made up of many cells. A liquid called the electrolyte is found in each cell. This liquid is made up of billions of positive and negative charges.

Two rods made of different materials are submerged in the electrolyte in each cell. These rods are called electrodes. A chemical reaction in the electrolyte sends positive particles to one electrode and negative particles to the other.

When a wire is connected to the two electrodes, current flows along the wire. This current can be used to light a bulb. When the chemicals in the cell have been used up, the current no longer flows.

Parts Of A Dry Cell Battery

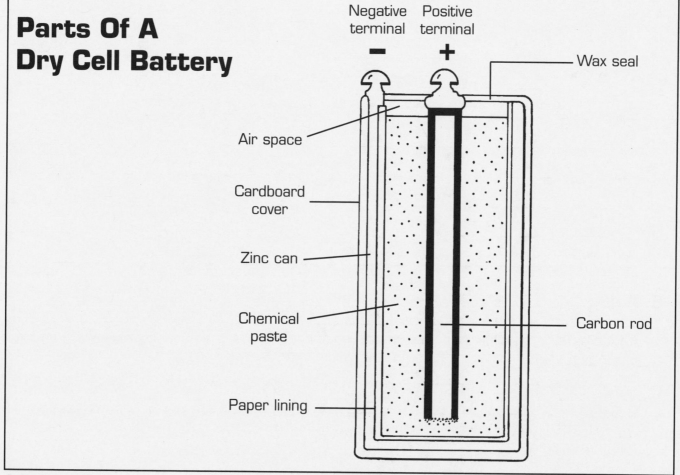

Negative terminal Positive terminal

− +

Wax seal

Air space

Cardboard cover

Zinc can

Chemical paste

Paper lining

Carbon rod

PITCH AND VOLUME SCALES

PITCH

Frequency (Vibrations Per Second)	Examples
16	lower limit of human hearing
20–200	deep bass tones (27= lowest note on piano)
256–512	"middle" musical scale (middle C to C above the staff)
525–3000	normal conversation
4000	about the highest musical tone
8000	high-pitched, shrill tones
20,000	upper limit of human hearing
30,000	upper limit of hearing for dogs and cats
100,000	upper limit of hearing for bats

VOLUME

Decibels	Examples
0	threshold of hearing
10	ordinary breathing
11–20	whispers
21–30	ordinary household sounds
31–40	activities such as turning pages of newspapers
41–50	automobile engines & vacuum cleaners
51–60	noisy stores
61–70	ordinary conversation
71–80	heavy street traffic
81–90	trains & subways
91–100	boiler factories, air drills, riveters
101–110	thunderclaps, jet engines
120	threshold of pain

Science Yellow Pages, Rev. Ed.

PHYSICAL SCIENCE GLOSSARY

Acceleration — the rate at which the velocity of an object changes

Acid — a chemical substance that reacts with metals to release hydrogen

Atom — a tiny particle of matter consisting of a nucleus that contains protons and neutrons and an electron cloud that contains electrons

Atomic Number — the number of protons in the nucleus of an atom which identifies the kind of atom

Boiling — The process in which particles of a liquid change to gas, travel to the surface of the liquid, and pass into the air

Catalyst — a substance that speeds up chemical reactions, but is not changed by the reaction

Celsius — a temperature scale used in the metric system in which water freezes at 0 degrees and boils at 100 degrees

Chemical Change — a change in which atoms and molecules form or break chemical bonds

Chemical Equation — a description of a chemical reaction using symbols and formulas

Chemical Formula — the combination of chemical symbols used as a shorthand for the name of a compound

Chemical Property — a property that describes the behavior of a substance when it reacts with other substances

Chemical Reaction — a change that produces one or more new substances

Chemical Symbol — the shorthand way of writing the name of an element

Chemistry — the study of matter

Coefficient — a number that tells how many molecules of a substance are needed or produced in a reaction

Compound — a substance made up of two or more elements

Conductor — a material that transmits or carries electricity

Conservation of Energy — the principle that energy cannot be made or destroyed, but only changed in form, and that the total energy in a physical system cannot be increased or diminished

Crystal — a solidified form of a substance in which the atoms or molecules are arranged in a definite pattern

Density — the ratio of the mass of an object to its volume

Direct Current — electric current that moves in one direction only

Electron — a negatively charged atomic particle

Emulsion — a suspension of two liquids

Fahrenheit — the temperature scale in which the freezing point of water is 32 degrees and the boiling point of water is 212 degrees

Fulcrum — the point on which a lever is supported

Galvanometer — a tool used for measuring very small electrical currents

Gas — the form of matter that has no definite shape or volume

Gravity — the force of attraction between objects and the earth

Heterogeneous Mixture — a mixture in which the composition is not the same throughout

Inertia — the property of matter to resist changes in motion

Insoluble — that which cannot be dissolved

Ion — an electrically charged atom which has lost or gained one or more electrons in a chemical reaction

Liquid — the form of matter that has a definite volume but no definite shape

Luminous Objects — objects that give off their own light

Mass — the amount of matter in an object

Matter — anything that has mass and takes up space

Mixture — a substance containing two or more ingredients which are not in fixed proportions, do not lose their individual characteristics of the element or compound

Molecule — the smallest particle of an element or compound that can exist in the free state and still retain the characteristics of the element or compound

Negative Charge — the charge of an atom having an excess of electrons (an electron has a negative charge)

Neutral — neither positively nor negatively charged; neither acidic nor basic

Neutron — a neutral atomic particle

Non-electrolyte — a substance that will not make water conduct electricity

Nucleus — the center of an atom which contains protons and neutrons

Oxidation — the union of a substance with oxygen; the process of increasing the positive capacity of an element or the negative capacity of an element to combine with another to form molecules; the process of removing electrons from atoms or ions

Physical Change — a change in which chemical bonds are not formed or broken and no new substance is produced

Physical Property — a property that distinguishes one type of matter from another and can be observed without changing the identity of the substance

Physics — the study of different forms of energy

Positive Charge — the charge of an atom having an excess of protons (protons have a positive charge)

Precipitate — an undissolved solid that usually sinks to the bottom of a mixture

Property — a quality that describes or characterizes an object

Proton — a positively charged particle found in the nucleus of an atom

Pure Substance — a substance that contains only one kind of material, has definite properties, and is the same throughout

Refraction — the bending of light as it passes from one medium to another

Suspension — a cloudy mixture of two or more substances that settles on standing

EARTH & SPACE SCIENCE
45 STUDENT INVESTIGATIONS

1. What are the four "layers" of the earth?

2. What is the "inside" of the earth like?

3. What is a topographic map and how do you read it?

4. How are igneous, sedimentary, and metamorphic rocks formed?

5. How are minerals formed?

6. How are crystals formed and why are they different shapes?

7. How can one identify a mineral?

8. What can be learned by studying minerals?

9. How do winds and waves change the earth's surface?

10. What land shapes can be formed by running water?

11. What causes earthquakes?

12. What causes a volcano to erupt?

13. How many different landforms can you name and describe?

14. What factors affect weathering?

15. How does the soil of various climates differ?

16. What kinds of formations and features are formed by groundwater?

17. What are fossils and how are they formed?

18. What is the geologic time scale?

19. What is the water cycle?

20. What is known about the gases in the air?

21. What is air pressure and how is it measured?

22. How are these caused differently: fog, frost, sleet, hail, dew, rain, and snow?

23. What is the difference between these: blizzard, tornado, cyclone, hurricane?

24. How can one accurately record daily weather conditions?

25. What are the different kinds of clouds?

26. What are clouds made of and how are they formed?

27. How does weather affect the earth and its inhabitants?

28. How does one read a weather map?

29. What factors determine climate?

30. How are climates classified?

31. How is relative humidity measured?

32. What causes ocean waves?

33. What causes ocean currents?

34. What causes different tides?

35. How does the ocean floor look?

36. What elements does ocean water contain?

37. What kinds of life are found in the ocean?

38. What causes air, water, and noise pollution?

39. What are the tools of astronomy?

40. What are constellations?

41. What can be learned from studying stars?

42. How does a solar or lunar eclipse occur?

43. What is known about the inner and outer planets?

44. How are stars born, and how do they die?

45. What is the difference between a black hole and a wormhole?

GASES IN THE ATMOSPHERE

Gas	Chemical Symbol	Percentage	Uses
Nitrogen	N_2	78%	used in fertilizers, amino acids, nitroglycerin
Oxygen	O_2	21%	needed by most living things; used as fuel for rockets in its liquid form
Argon	Ar	0.94%	used in light bulbs
Carbon dioxide	CO_2	0.03%	used by plants in making food
Water vapor	H_2O	0–4%	needed by all living things
Neon	Ne	trace	used in rockets and weather balloons
Helium	He	trace	used in advertising signs
Methane	CH_4	trace	used in industry, home heating, and gas (for cooking)
Krypton	Kr	trace	used in fluorescent lights
Hydrogen	H_2	trace	used as a fuel; used to cool electric generators and motors; used in the production of ammonia
Xenon	Xe	trace	used to fill flash bulbs
Ozone	O_3	trace	used for disinfecting, cleaning and removing odors

TYPES OF CLOUDS

Name	Description	Weather Prediction
Cumulus	turret-shaped tops, flat bottoms	fair weather
Cumulonimbus	thunderheads (large, dark cumulus)	thunderstorm
Stratus	smooth layers of low clouds	chance of drizzle or snow
Stratocumulus	piles of clouds in layers	chance of drizzle or snow
Nimbostratus	smooth layers of dark gray clouds	continuous precipitation
Altostratus	thick sheets of gray or blue clouds	rain or snow
Altocumulus	piles of clouds in waves	rain or snow
Cirrus	feather-like clouds (made of ice crystals)	fair weather
Cirrostratus	thin sheets of clouds (causes halo around the sun or moon)	rain or snow within 24 hours
Cirrocumulus	"cottony" clouds in waves	fair weather

Science Yellow Pages, Rev. Ed.

THE BEAUFORT SCALE OF WIND STRENGTH

Beaufort Number	Wind Name	Wind Speed (km/hr)	Description
1	light air	1–5	wind direction shown by smoke drift; weather vanes inactive
2	light breeze	6–11	wind felt on face; leaves move slightly; weather vanes active; smoke does not rise vertically
3	gentle breeze	12–19	leaves and small twigs move constantly; flags blow
4	moderate breeze	20–28	dust and paper blow about; twigs and thin branches move
5	fresh breeze	29–38	small trees sway; white caps form on lakes
6	strong breeze	39–49	large branches move; telegraph wires whistle; umbrellas are hard to find
7	moderate gale	50–61	large trees sway; it's somewhat difficult to walk
8	fresh gale	62–74	twigs break off of trees; walking against the wind is very difficult; possible damage to property
9	strong gale	75–88	slight damage to buildings; shingles are blown off roof
10	whole gale	89–102	trees are uprooted; much damage to buildings
11	storm	103–117	widespread damage (rarely occurs inland)
12	hurricane	more than 117	extreme destruction

THE CYCLES OF NATURE

The Water Cycle

The Rock Cycle

IGNEOUS ROCKS

SEDIMENTARY ROCKS

METAMORPHIC ROCKS

Science Yellow Pages, Rev. Ed.

The Oxygen-Carbon Dioxide Cycle

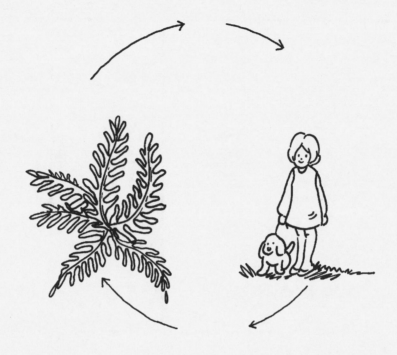

The Nitrogen Cycle

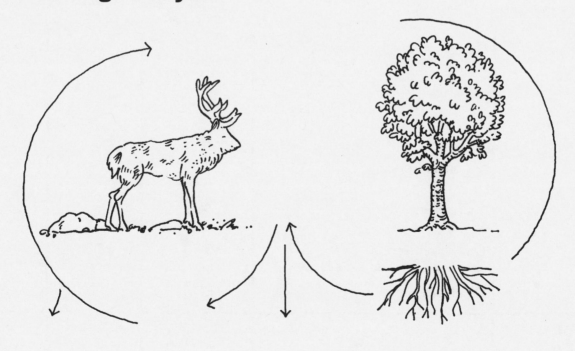

THE GEOLOGIC TIME SCALE

ERA	PERIOD/EPOCH		BEGINNING (millions of years ago)	DURATION (millions of years)	DURATION OF ERAS
Cenozoic Era	Quaternary Period	Recent Epoch	began 10,000 years ago		70 million years
		Pleistocene Epoch	2.5	2.5	
	Tertiary Period	Pliocene Epoch	14	11.5	
		Miocene Epoch	25	11	
		Oligocene Epoch	35	10	
		Eocene Epoch	55	20	
		Paleocene Epoch	70	15	
Mesozoic Era	Cretaceous Period		135	65	160 million years
	Jurassic period		180	45	
	Triassic Period		230	50	
Paleozoic Era	Permian Period		285	55	370 million years
	Carboniferous Period	Pennsylvanian Epoch	325	40	
		Mississippian Epoch	350	25	
	Devonian Period		410	60	
	Silurian Period		430	20	
	Ordovician Period		500	70	
	Cambrian Period		600	100	
Precambrian Era			4.6 billion years	almost 4 billion years	

Science Yellow Pages, Rev. Ed.

BIOME CHARACTERISTICS

Biome	Climate	Common Plants	Common Animals	Average Yearly Rainfall
coniferous forest	cool and moist on mountains; mild winters and heavy rainfalls in coastal areas	conifers: cedars, hemlocks, pines, redwoods	bears, mountain lions, wolves, elks	more than 50 cm
deciduous forest	moist with cold winters and warm summers	broadleaf deciduous trees: elms, maples, oaks	raccoons, squirrels, small birds, deer	more than 75 cm
desert	extremely dry	cacti, fleshy plants, grasses, small-leaved shrubs	lizards, snakes, small rodents (wood rats, kangaroo rats)	less than 25 cm
grasslands	mild temperatures and sub-humid	grasses and herbaceous plants	antelopes, buffaloes, wolves, coyotes	25–75 cm
tropical rain forest	warm and wet all year	broadleaf evergreens, palms, tree ferns, climbing vines	bats, lizards, snakes, monkeys, colorful birds	more than 200 cm
tundra	extremely cold and dry; permafrost	lichens, shrubs, grasslike plants	arctic foxes, polar bears, caribou, wolves, migratory birds	20 cm

THE MAKE-UP OF THE EARTH

Characteristics of the Earth's Layers

Layer	Chemical Makeup	Average Thickness	Percentage of Total Mass of the Earth
Crust	oxygen, silicone, aluminum, iron, sodium, magnesium, potassium	35 km continents 7 km oceans	0.4
Mantle	silicone, oxygen, aluminum, iron	2900 km	68.1
Outer Core	iron and nickel (liquid)	2200 km	31.5 (outer and inner core combined)
Inner Core	iron and nickel (solid)	1270 km	

Elements In The Earth's Crust

Element	Percentage in Crust
Oxygen	46.60
Silicone	27.72
Aluminum	8.13
Iron	5.00
Calcium	3.63
Sodium	2.83
Potassium	2.59
Magnesium	2.09
Titanium	0.04
Hydrogen	0.14
Other	1.23
TOTAL	**100.00**

Elements In The Ocean

Element	Percentage of Total
Oxygen & Hydrogen	96.5
Chlorine	1.9
Sodium	1.1
Magnesium, Sulfur, Calcium, Potassium, Bromine, Carbon, Strontium, Silicone, Fluorine, Aluminum, Phosphorus, Iodine	0.5
TOTAL	**100.00**

Science Yellow Pages, Rev. Ed.

COMMON MINERALS AND THEIR USES

MINERAL	USES
Alum	used in cosmetics and dyes and also used for purification
Bauxite	a source of aluminum
Calcite	used in medicine and toothpaste; also found in marble and limestone (used as building materials)
Corundum	used to make emery boards and to grind and polish metals
Feldspar	used to make pottery, china and glass
Graphite	used in pencils and as a lubricant in small machines, clocks and locks
Halite	rock salt
Hematite	a source of iron
Jade	used to make vases, figurines, jewelry, etc.
Malachite	used to make table tops and jewelry
Quartz	used in radios, televisions, and radar equipment
Sulfur	used to make matches, medicine, rubber, and gunpowder
Talc	used to line furnaces, insulate electrical wires, make powder, crayons, soap, paint

CRYSTAL SHAPES

Type & Number of Surfaces	Shapes of Surfaces	Examples
Cubic 6	all are square	alum, pyrite, garnet, gold, sodium chloride, silver, diamond
Hexagonal 8	2 are hexagons, 6 are rectangles (angles of rectangles are right angles)	ice, ruby, sapphire, quartz, emerald, apatite
Monoclinic 6	4 are rectangles, 2 are parallelograms, 16 angles are right angles, 8 angles are not right angles	sugar, gypsum, borax
Orthorhombic 6	3 pairs of rectangles, each pair a different size, corner angles are right angles	topaz, Epsom salt, rhombic sulfur
Rhombohedral 6	all are rhombuses, no right angles	calcite
Tetragonal 6	4 are rectangles, 2 are squares, corner angles are right angles	white tin, zircon
Triclinic 6	all are parallelograms, no right angles at corners	boric acid, copper sulfate

COLOR SORTING KEY FOR MINERALS IN ROCKS

EXTERNAL COLOR	STREAK TEST	MINERAL
blue-green	white	apatite
blue or white	white	calcite
brass yellow	greenish-black	chalcopyrite
lead gray	lead gray	galena
gray, red-brown	red-brown	hematite
brown	ochre yellow	limonite
black	black	magnetite
bright green	pale green	malachite
pale yellow	greenish-black	pyrite
gray or green	white	talc

HARDNESS SCALES

The hardness of a mineral is its ability to resist scratching. A German mineralogist named Frederick Mohs developed a scale of hardness for minerals which arranges common minerals according to the hardness of each. The Field Hardness Scale is helpful for testing hardness when the minerals in the Mohs scale are not available, such as in fieldwork.

Mohs Hardness Scale

MINERAL	HARDNESS	HARDNESS TEST
Talc	1	softest, can be scratched by your fingernail
Gypsum	2	soft, can also be scratched by fingernail (but cannot be scratched by talc)
Calcite	3	can be scratched by a penny
Fluorite	4	can be scratched by a steel knife or a nail file, but not easily
Apatite	5	can be scratched by a steel knife or a nail file
Feldspar	6	knife cannot scratch it, and it can scratch glass
Quartz	7	scratches glass and steel
Topaz	8	can scratch quartz
Corundum	9	can scratch topaz
Diamond	10	can scratch all others

Field Hardness Scale

HARDNESS	COMMON TEST
1	can be easily scratched with a fingernail
2	can be scratched by fingernail
3	can be scratched by a penny
4	can be scratched easily by a knife, but will not scratch glass
5	difficult to scratch with a knife, barely scratches glass
6	can be scratched by a steel file, easily scratches glass
7	scratches a steel file and glass

Science Yellow Pages, Rev. Ed.

SOLAR SYSTEM STATISTICS

PLANET	AVERAGE DISTANCE FROM SUN (millions of km)	DIAMETER (km)	PERIOD of REVOLUTION (in Earth Time) Days and Years	ROTATION (in Earth Time)	MOONS
Mercury	58	4,880	88 years	59 days	0
Venus	108	12,104	225	243 days	0
Earth	150	12,756	365	24 hours	1
Mars	228	6,787	1.88	24.6 hours	2
Jupiter	778	142,800	11.86	9.9 hours	16
Saturn	1,427	120,000	29.47	10.3 hours	17
Uranus	2,869	51,800	84.01	10.7 hours	5
Neptune	4,486	49,500	164.8	15 hours	2
Pluto	5,900	6,000	248.4	6.4 days	0

PHASES OF THE MOON

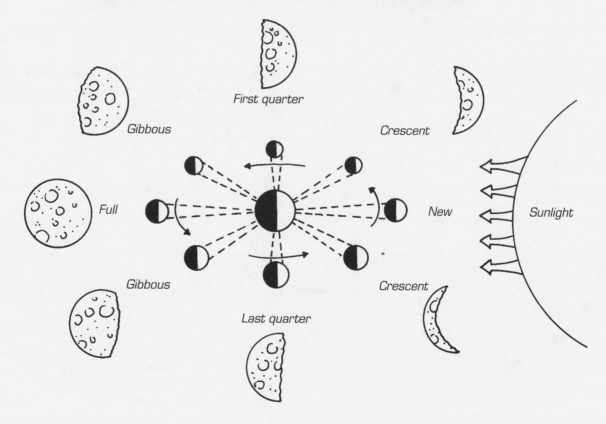

First quarter

Gibbous

Crescent

Full

New

Sunlight

Gibbous

Crescent

Last quarter

THE NIGHT SKY IN EVERY SEASON

Winter

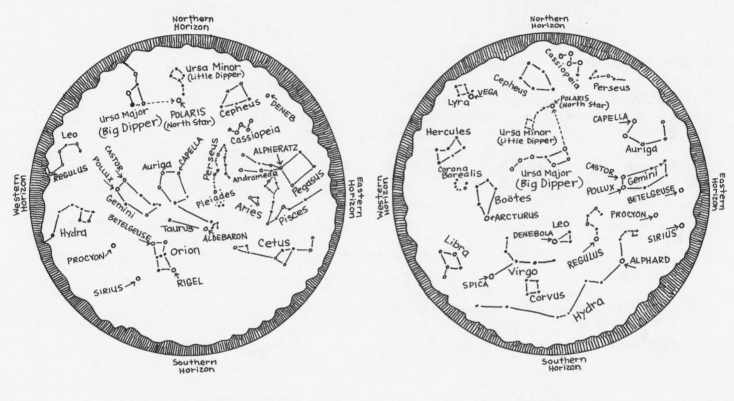

Spring

Summer

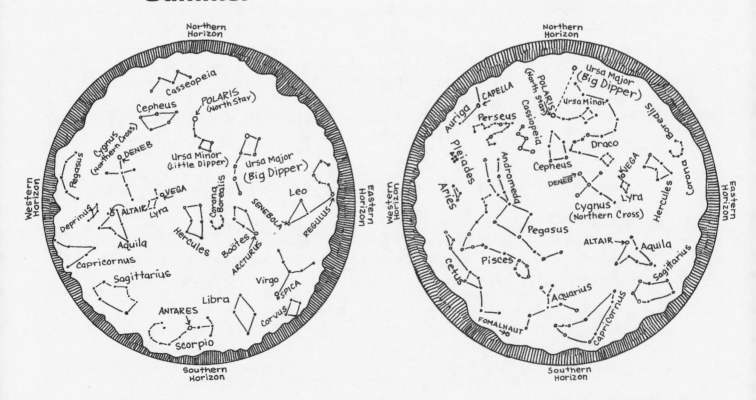

Fall

Science Yellow Pages, Rev. Ed.

EARTH & SPACE SCIENCE GLOSSARY

Abrasion — the wearing away of rocks by rubbing and scraping

Absolute Magnitude — the measure of a star's actual brightness

Abyss — ocean depths of 2000–6000 meters

Air Mass — a body of air that has the same properties as the region over which it develops

Anemometer — an instrument used to measure wind speed

Apparent Motion — the motion of an object relative to the position of its observer

Aquifers — permeable rocks containing water

Arid Climate — a climate in which the plants receive much less rainfall than they require

Asteroids — numerous small planets with orbits between those of Mars and Jupiter

Astronomy — the study of the stars, planets, and other heavenly bodies

Atmosphere — the gaseous mass that surrounds any star or planet

Axis — an imaginary line around which something spins

Barometer — an instrument used to measure air pressure

Bedrock — the solid rock found under soil

Comet — a heavenly body consisting of rocks and gases that orbits the sun

Conglomerate — sedimentary rock made of pebbles and gravel cemented together by clay

Convection Current — the movement of material within a fluid caused by uneven temperature; the upward movement of warm air and the downward movement of cool air

Crust — the outermost layer of Earth, extending to a depth of about 35 km

Density Currents — currents of water that move up and down in the ocean

Diurnal — an event occurring once a day; usually referring to tides

Drag — a force of friction that resists the movement of a body through a fluid medium

Elevation — the distance of a point above or below sea level

Full Moon — moon phase occurring when Earth is between the sun and the moon, with the sun shining on the moon so that it is visible from Earth

Galaxy — a large grouping of millions of stars

Gemstones — a mineral or petrified substance that can be used as a gem when cut and polished

Geologic Time Scale — a history of the earth based on observations of rocks and fossils

Geyser — a spring from which boiling water and steam shoot into the air at intervals

Glacier — a moving river of ice and snow

Gravity — the force of attraction that exists between all objects in the universe

Hydrosphere — all of the water on the face of the earth

Igneous Rock — rocks formed from the cooling of hot, molten magma

Latitude — distance, measured in degrees, north or south of the equator

Longitude — distance, measured in degrees, east or west of the prime meridian

Lunar Eclipse — the partial or total obscuring of the moon when the earth comes directly between the sun and the moon

Magma — liquid or molten rock deep inside the earth

Mantle — the thick layer of the earth between the crust and the core

Meridian — imaginary lines running from the North Pole to the South Pole

Meteor — the flash of light that occurs when a meteoroid is heated by its entry into the earth's atmosphere (a shooting or falling star)

Meteorite — the part of a meteoroid that passes through the atmosphere and falls to the earth's surface

Meteoroid — any of the small, solid bodies that travel through outer space and are seen as meteors when they enter earth's atmosphere

Mineral — an inorganic substance that occurs naturally in the earth and has a specific set of physical properties

Mountain — a raised part of the earth's surface with an elevation of at least 600 meters higher than the surrounding land

Neap Tides — low tides that occur when the sun, Earth, and moon form a right angle

New Moon — phase of the moon in which the side of the moon facing Earth is dark

Orbit — the path of one object in freefall around another object in space

Penumbra — a partial shadow formed during an eclipse

Period — a subdivision of a geologic era (periods are combined to form eras and are subdivided into epochs)

Phases — any of the recurring stages of changes in the appearance of the moon or a planet

Plain — a large, flat area with an elevation that differs little from that of the surrounding area

Planet — an object in space that reflects light from a nearby star around which it revolves

Plateau — a large, flat area with at least one side having a sharply higher elevation than that of the surrounding area

Plates — rigid blocks of Earth's crust and upper mantle

Plate Tectonics — a theory that explains movements of continents and changes in Earth's crust caused by internal forces

Precipitation — the falling of water or ice formed by condensation

Prehistoric — before recorded history

Richter Scale — a means for measuring the magnitude of earthquakes

Sandstone — sedimentary rock made of sand

Satellite — a small planet that revolves around a larger one; a man-made object put into orbit around some heavenly body

Schist — a metamorphic rock containing parallel layers of flaky minerals

Sedimentary Rocks — rocks formed by the cementing together of materials

Seismograph — an instrument that measures movements in the earth's crust

Shale — sedimentary rock made of mud and clay that splits easily into thin layers

Sill — igneous rock that has solidified between and parallel to the layers of rock in the earth's crust

Slate — a metamorphic rock that is made from shale and that breaks in flat sheets

Solar Eclipse — an eclipse that occurs when Earth is in the moon's shadow

Spring Tides — tides that occur when the sun, moon, and Earth align

Stratosphere — the second layer of the atmosphere (above the troposphere) which extends six to fifteen miles above the earth's surface and where the temperature is fairly constant

Stratus Clouds — clouds that extend in long, low, gray layers

Sunspot — a temporarily cooler area of the sun that appears as a dark spot on the surface

Telescope — an instrument which makes distant objects appear closer and larger

Umbra — an inner, complete shadow formed during an eclipse

Weathering — the process by which surface rocks and other materials are broken down by wind, water, and ice

Wind — movements of air parallel to Earth's surface

LIFE SCIENCE
45 STUDENT INVESTIGATIONS

1. Why do living things need air, food, and water?

2. How do cells, tissues, and organs work together?

3. How do plant cells differ from animal cells?

4. How are living things classified?

5. How do plants get energy?

6. How does pollination work?

7. Why are roots, stems and leaves important to plants?

8. What is an ecosystem?

9. How do light, air, water, and temperature affect germination?

10. How is gravity related to growth?

11. How is a food chain different from a food web?

12. What are the differences between different biomes?

13. What happens when an ecosystem gets out of balance?

14. How do animals differ from plants?

15. How do insects develop?

16. Do ants have organized communities?

17. How is an insect different from an arachnid?

18. What special adaptations do various plants and animals have for survival?

19. How do various animals take care of their young?

20. What is meant by "the survival of the fittest?"

21. How do green plants make oxygen?

22. How can someone test foods for fat, proteins, and carbohydrates?

23. How does the human eye work?

24. How does the human ear work?

25. How does the human sense of smell work?

26. How does a tongue taste food?

27. How does food give the body energy?

28. What foods contain high amounts of acids?

29. What foods contain high amounts of bases?

30. How can the five senses be "fooled?"

31. What are reflexes?

32. Why is the skin an important sense organ?

33. How do people react to the changes around them?

34. How does a broken bone heal?

35. How does food turn into energy for the body to use?

36. What are inherited characteristics?

37. What is genetic engineering?

38. What benefits might result from the mapping of human genes?

39. How does the body fight disease?

40. In what ways can an infection spread?

41. What kinds of bacteria are helpful?

42. What kinds of bacteria are harmful?

43. What is a virus?

44. How does a vaccination work to protect the body from disease?

45. How do drugs, alcohol, and tobacco affect the body?

SYSTEM OF CLASSIFICATION FOR ORGANISMS

A Swedish scientist named Carolus Linnaeus developed the modern classification system for grouping organisms in the 1700s. This system involves seven classification groups. This branch of science that deals with classification is called taxonomy.

CLASSIFICATION CHART

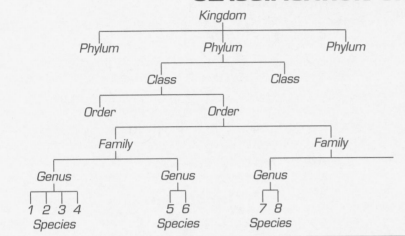

Example: DOG

Kingdom — Animal

Phylum — Chordata

Class — Mammalia

Order — Carnivora

Family — Canidae

Genus — Canis

Species — Canis familiaris

PARTS OF A PLANT CELL

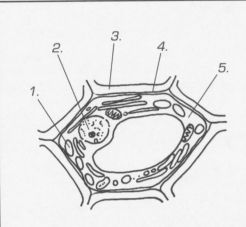

1. **Chloroplast** — the oval body in a green plant cell which contains the chlorophyll
2. **Nucleus** — the central mass of protoplasm, which contains most of the hereditary material necessary for such functions as growth, reproduction, etc.
3. **Wall** — the rigid covering of the cell that contains cellulose and other substances
4. **Membrane** — a very thin living membrane surrounding the cytoplasm
5. **Cytoplasm** — the protoplasm (essential living matter) of a cell that is found outside the nucleus

PARTS OF AN ANIMAL CELL

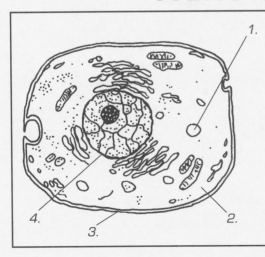

1. **Vacuole** — a clear, fluid-filled cavity within the plasma membrane believed to discharge excess water or wastes
2. **Cytoplasm** — the protoplasm (essential living matter) of a cell that is found outside the nucleus
3. **Cell Membrane** — a very thin living membrane surrounding the cytoplasm
4. **Nucleus** — the central mass of protoplasm that contains most of the hereditary material necessary for such functions as growth, reproduction, etc.

THE PARTS OF A FLOWER

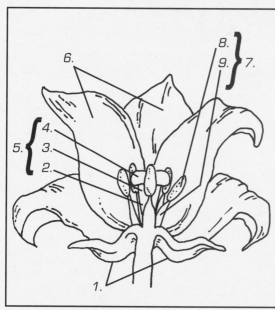

1. **Sepals** — the outer protective, leaf-like parts of the flower
2. **Ovary** — the enlarged hollow part of the pistil which contains the ovules
3. **Style** — the slender, stalk-like part between the stigma and the ovary
4. **Stigma** — the free upper tip of the style on which pollen falls and develops
5. **Pistil** — the seed-bearing organ
6. **Petals** — the leafy, protective parts of the flower
7. **Stamen** — a pollen-bearing organ made up of a slender stalk and a pollen sac
8. **Anther** — the part of the stamen that contains pollen
9. **Filament** — the stalk of the stamen bearing the anther

SOME COMMON POISONOUS PLANTS

Plant	Dangers
Autumn crocus or meadow saffron	intense thirst, burning of throat, vomiting; possible death from respiratory failure
Bird of Paradise	severe poisoning if ingested
Black locust	Seeds can cause dullness and depression; vomiting and weak pulse may occur if ingested.
Buttercup	Irritant juices may severely injure the digestive system.
Crownflower	Sap can cause severe eye injury.
Elderberry	Children have been poisoned by using the pithy stems for blowguns. The result is nausea and an upset digestive system.
Elephant ear	Intense pain around lips, mouth, and tongue if chewed; If base of tongue swells and blocks air passage, death can result
Hyacinth, daffodil, narcissus	Bulbs may cause nausea, vomiting and diarrhea if ingested; may be fatal.
Lily of the Valley	Roots, leaves and fruit can stimulate the heart (similar to digitalis).
Oak	Chewing of leaves or acorns gradually affects kidneys; symptoms appear only after several days or weeks.
Philodendron	skin rash requiring long-term medical care; swelling of mouth and throat if ingested
Red pepper, chili	burns skin and mouth; Large doses may cause severe poisoning.
Rhododendron	intense pain, diarrhea, and discomfort
Rhubarb	Ingestion of large amounts of leaf blades can cause convulsions, coma, and death.
Wisteria	Seeds and pods cause mild to severe digestive upset.
Yew	violent gastrointestinal distress; Ingestion also causes quick pulse, fainting, convulsions, and death.

ANIMAL GROUPINGS
AND OFFSPRING NAMES

Animal	Group Name	Offspring
bear	colony	cub
beaver	swarm	kit
cat	flock, cluster	kitten
chicken	clutch, brood	chick
cow	pack, herd	calf
dog	brace, flock, pack, kennel	pup, puppy, whelp
elephant	gang, herd	calf
fox	skulk	cub
goat	cast	kid
goose	flock, gaggle	gosling
hawk	drift	eyas
kangaroo	pride	joey
lion	sord, monkey, pride	cub
pig	drove, litter	piglet, farrow, shoat
rabbit	colony, nest	bunny
seal	pod	pup
sheep	drove, flock	lamb
turkey	rafter	poult
whale	gam, pod	calf
wolf	pack, rout	cub, whelp

Science Yellow Pages, Rev. Ed.

SELECTED ENDANGERED ANIMAL SPECIES OF NORTH AMERICA

Mammals

Bat, gray
Bat, Indiana
Bat, Mariana fruit
Bat, Virginia big-eared
Bear, American black
Bear, grizzly
Caribou, woodland
Deer, Columbian white-tail
Deer, key
Ferret, black-footed
Fox, San Joaquin kit
Jaguar
Kangaroo rat, Fresno
Kangaroo rat, giant
Kangaroo rat, Morrow Bay
Kangaroo rat, Tipton
Lynx, Canada
Manatee, West Indian
Mountain beaver, Point Arena
Mouse, Alabama beach
Mouse, Anastasia Island beach
Mouse, Key Largo cotton
Mouse, Pacific pocket
Mouse, salt marsh harvest
Ocelot
Otter, southern sea
Panther, Florida
Prairie dog, Utah
Pronghorn, Sonoran
Puma
Puma, eastern
Rabbit, Lower Keys marsh
Rice rat
Sea lion, Steller
Seal, Caribbean monk
Seal, Guadalupe fur
Seal, Hawaiian monk
Sheep, bighorn
Squirrel, Mount Graham red
Squirrel, northern Idaho ground
Vole, Florida salt marsh
Whale, blue
Whale, bowhead,
Whale, finback
Whale, humpback
Whale, right
Whale, sperm
Wolf, gray
Wolf, red
Woodrat, Key Largo

Birds

Akepa, Hawaii
Albatross, short-tailed
Blackbird, yellow-shouldered
Bobwhite, masked
Broadbill, Guam
Cahow
Caracara
Condor, California
Coot, Hawaiian
Crane, Mississippi sandhill
Crane, whooping
Creeper, Hawaii
Creeper, Molokai
Creeper, Oahu
Crow, Hawaiian
Crow, Mariana
Curlew, Eskimo
Duck, Hawaiian
Duck, Laysan
Eagle, Greenland white-tailed
Eagle, bald
Eider, bespeckled
Falcon, northern aplomado
Finch, Laysan
Goose, Hawaiian
Hawk, Hawaiian
Hawk, Puerto Rican
Honeycreeper, crested
Jay, Florida scrub
Kingfisher, Guam
Kite, Everglade
Mallard, Mariana
Owl, Mexican spotted
Owl, northern spotted
Parrotbill, Maui
Pelican, brown
Rail, California Clapper
Sparrow, Cape Sable Seaside
Stilt, Hawaiian
Stork, wood
Swiftlet, Mariana gray
Tern, California least
Tern, least
Thrush, large Kauai
Warbler, Bachman's
Warbler, Kirtland's
Warbler, nightingale reed
White-eye, bridled
Woodpecker, ivory-billed
Woodpecker, red-cockaded

Reptiles

Alligator, American
Boa, Mona
Boa, Puerto Rican
Boa, Virgin Islands tree
Crocodile, American
Gecko, Monito
Iguana, Mona ground
Lizard, blunt-nosed leopard
Lizard, island night
Rattlesnake, New Mexican
  ridge-nosed
Snake, Atlantic salt marsh
Snake, eastern indigo
Snake, San Francisco garter
Tortoise, desert
Turtle, green sea
Turtle, loggerhead sea

Amphibians

Coqui, golden
Frog, California red-legged
Salamander, desert slender
Salamander, flatwoods
Salamander, Texas blind
Toad, arroyo
Toad, Houston
Toad, Wyoming

Fish

Catfish, Yawui
Cavefish, Alabama
Chub, bonytail
Chub, Oregon
Dace, desert
Darter, amber
Goby, tidewater
Minnow, Devils River
Pupfish, desert
Salmon, Atlantic
Salmon, chinook
Salmon, chum,
Salmon, Coho
Salmon, sockeye
Smelt, delta
Sucker, razorback
Trout, Apache
Trout, bull
Trout, greenback cutthroat

DIAGRAMS OF THE FIVE SENSES

Human Ear

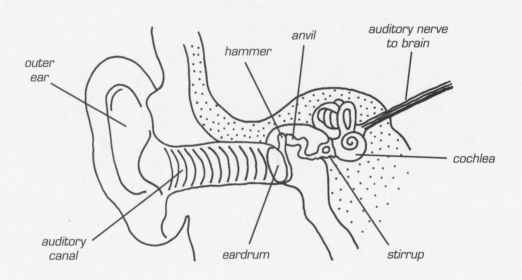

outer
ear

hammer

anvil

auditory nerve
to brain

cochlea

auditory
canal

eardrum

stirrup

Human Skin

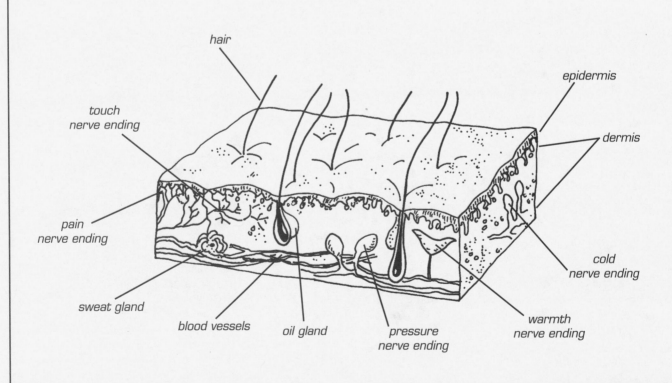

hair

epidermis

touch
nerve ending

dermis

pain
nerve ending

cold
nerve ending

sweat gland

blood vessels

oil gland

pressure
nerve ending

warmth
nerve ending

54

The Human Eye

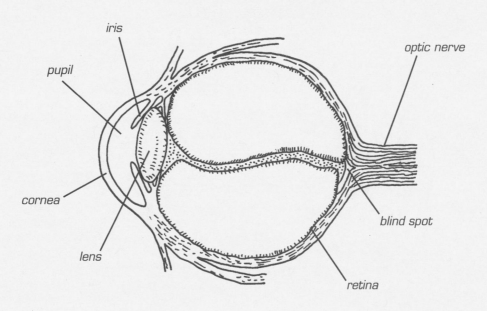

iris

pupil

optic nerve

cornea

blind spot

lens

retina

The Human Nose

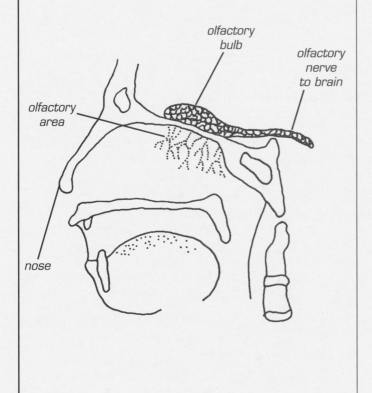

olfactory bulb

olfactory nerve to brain

olfactory area

nose

The Human Tongue

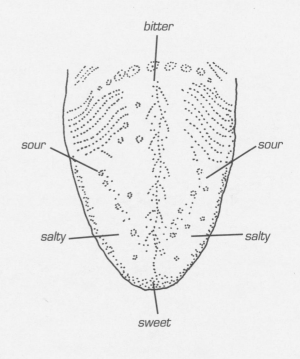

bitter

sour

sour

salty

salty

sweet

THE HUMAN ORGAN SYSTEMS

System	Function	Some Organs
Circulatory System	transports food, oxygen, and wastes throughout the body	heart, vessels, liver, kidneys
Digestive System	breaks down and processes food for use by the body	tongue, teeth, esophagus, salivary glands, liver, stomach, large intestine, small intestine, rectum, pancreas, gallbladder
Endocrine System	produces hormones that control body functions	pituitary gland, thyroid gland, parathyroid glands, hypothalamus, thymus gland, adrenal glands, pancreas, ovaries, testes
Excretory System	removes wastes from the body	skin, kidneys, bladder, ureters, urethra, lungs, intestines, rectum, anus
Integumentary System	outer body covering that protects the body	hair, skin, fingernails, toenails
Muscular System	supports and enables the body to move	muscles and tendons
Nervous System	carries messages back and forth to the brain and throughout the body to aid in controlling body function and in responding to the environment	brain, spinal chord, nerves
Reproductive System	produces sperm in males and eggs in females	ovaries, fallopian tubes, uterus, vagina, cervix, seminal vesicles, prostate gland, penis
Respiratory System	supplies body with a continuous supply of oxygen; removes carbon dioxide from the blood	nose, mouth, pharynx, larynx, trachea, epiglottis, lungs, bronchi, bronchioles, alveoli
Skeletal System	supports and protects the body	bones: cranium, maxilla, mandible, clavicle, scapula, sternum, ribs, humerus, vertebrae, radius, ulna, carpals, phalanges, pelvis, patella, femur, fibula, tibia, tarsals, metatarsals, phalanges

Science Yellow Pages, Rev. Ed.

THE HUMAN SKELETAL STRUCTURE AND BODY SYSTEMS

Skeletal System

Nervous System

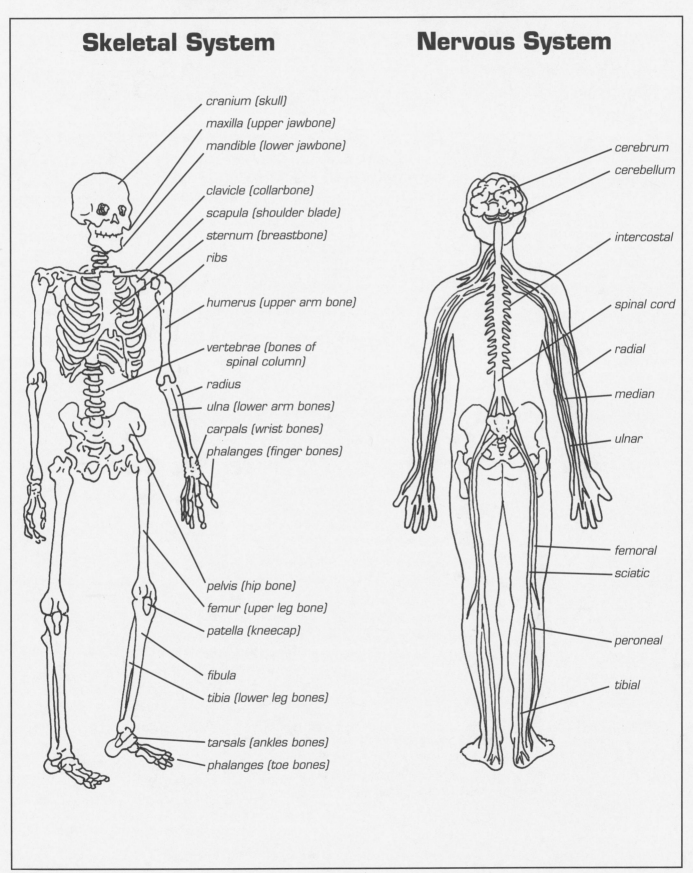

Skeletal System labels:
- cranium (skull)
- maxilla (upper jawbone)
- mandible (lower jawbone)
- clavicle (collarbone)
- scapula (shoulder blade)
- sternum (breastbone)
- ribs
- humerus (upper arm bone)
- vertebrae (bones of spinal column)
- radius
- ulna (lower arm bones)
- carpals (wrist bones)
- phalanges (finger bones)
- pelvis (hip bone)
- femur (uper leg bone)
- patella (kneecap)
- fibula
- tibia (lower leg bones)
- tarsals (ankles bones)
- phalanges (toe bones)

Nervous System labels:
- cerebrum
- cerebellum
- intercostal
- spinal cord
- radial
- median
- ulnar
- femoral
- sciatic
- peroneal
- tibial

Lymph System

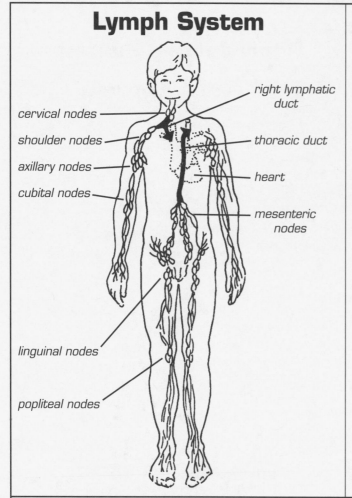

cervical nodes

shoulder nodes

axillary nodes

cubital nodes

right lymphatic duct

thoracic duct

heart

mesenteric nodes

linguinal nodes

popliteal nodes

Circulatory System

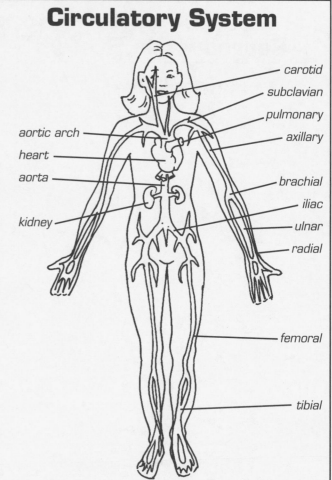

carotid

subclavian

pulmonary

axillary

aortic arch

heart

aorta

kidney

brachial

iliac

ulnar

radial

femoral

tibial

Respiratory System

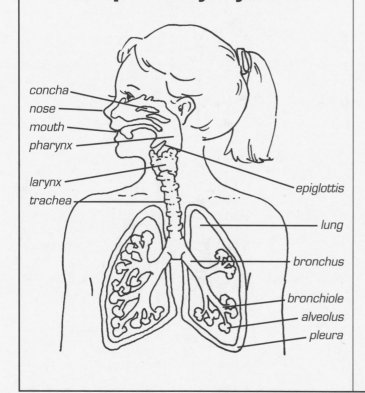

concha

nose

mouth

pharynx

larynx

trachea

epiglottis

lung

bronchus

bronchiole

alveolus

pleura

Endocrine System

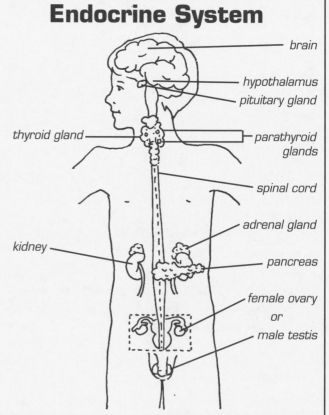

brain

hypothalamus

pituitary gland

thyroid gland

parathyroid glands

spinal cord

adrenal gland

kidney

pancreas

female ovary or male testis

58

Male Reproductive System

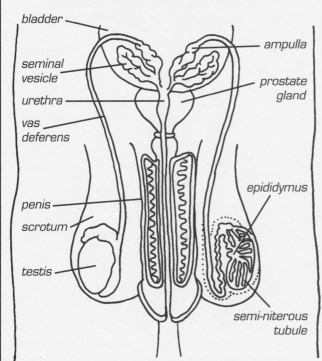

- bladder
- seminal vesicle
- urethra
- vas deferens
- penis
- scrotum
- testis
- ampulla
- prostate gland
- epididymus
- semi-niterous tubule

Female Reproductive System

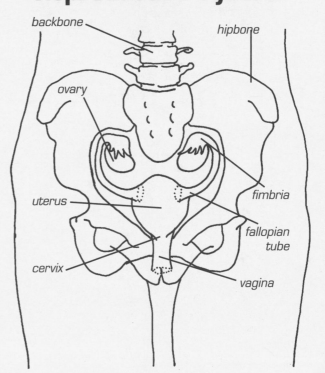

- backbone
- hipbone
- ovary
- uterus
- cervix
- fimbria
- fallopian tube
- vagina

Urinary System

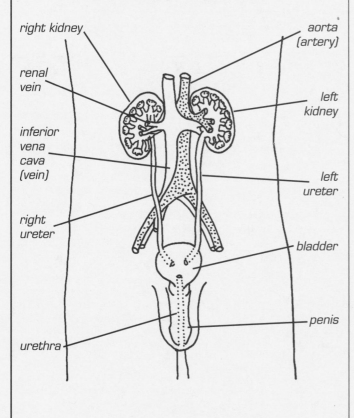

- right kidney
- renal vein
- inferior vena cava (vein)
- right ureter
- urethra
- aorta (artery)
- left kidney
- left ureter
- bladder
- penis

Digestive System

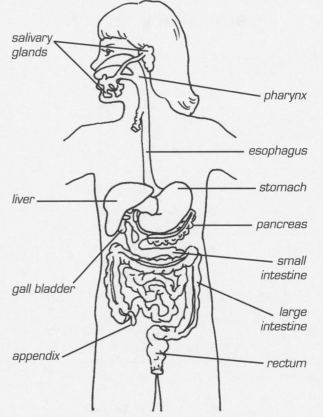

- salivary glands
- liver
- gall bladder
- appendix
- pharynx
- esophagus
- stomach
- pancreas
- small intestine
- large intestine
- rectum

THE FOOD PYRAMID

The Food Guide Pyramid was developed by the United States Department of Agriculture to guide people in making choices for a healthy diet. The pyramid shows the six major food groups and makes recommendations for the number of servings that should be eaten by people 6–70 years old. The basic idea of the pyramid is to show that the USDA recommends that more servings should be chosen from the foods at the bottom of the pyramid. The foods at the top of the pyramid should be eaten in the smallest amounts.

1. Fats, oils, and sweets group
Eat small amounts.

2. Meats, poultry, fish, dry beans, eggs, and nuts group
2–3 servings daily

3. Milk, yogurt, and cheese group
2–3 servings daily

4. Fruit group
2–4 servings daily

5. Vegetable group
3–5 servings daily

6. Bread, cereal, rice, and pasta group
6–11 servings daily

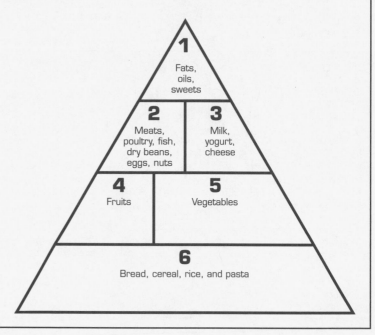

FOOD TESTS

Testing for protein:	Place a small amount of food in a test tube. Add a small amount of biuret solution. Protein is present if the solution changes from light blue to purple.
Testing for fats:	Rub the food on a piece of a brown paper bag. This will make a spot on the paper. If there are fats or oils in the food, the spot will not dry but will remain.
Testing for sugar:	Put a small piece of food into a test tube. Pour in enough Benedict's solution to cover the food. Heat the test tube gently. If the solution changes to green, yellow-orange, or brick red, then sugar is present
Testing for starch:	Add Lugol's solution to the food. If the solution turns blue-black, starch is present.
Testing for water:	Put a small piece of food in a dry test tube. Heat the test tube gently. If the food contains water, the water will be released as vapor. As the vapor touches the cooler surface of the test tube, small drops of water will form inside the tube.
Testing for minerals:	Put a piece of food in a clay dish. Heat the bottom of the dish until the food burns away. If a white or gray ash is left in the dish, the food contains minerals.

Science Yellow Pages, Rev. Ed.

IMPORTANT VITAMINS & MINERALS

Vitamins

Vitamin	Food Source	Needed For
A	green and yellow vegetables, eggs, fruits, liver	maintenance of skin, eggs, and mucous membranes; healthy bones and teeth; growth
B_1	whole-grain cereals, liver and other meats, nuts, vegetables	carbohydrate metabolism; functioning of heart and nerves, growth
B_2	milk, cheese, eggs, liver, fish, fowl, green vegetables	healthy skin; growth; eye functioning; carbohydrate functioning
B_{12}	liver and other meats, eggs, milk, green vegetables	proper development of red blood cells
C	citrus fruits, tomatoes, potatoes, leafy vegetables	healthy bones, teeth, and gums; growth; strength of blood vessels
D	milk, eggs, tuna, liver, sunlight	regulation of calcium and phosphorus metabolism; healthy bones and teeth
E	milk, butter, vegetable oils	maintenance of cell membranes
K	tomatoes, soybean oil, leafy vegetables, liver	blood clotting; normal liver functioning

Minerals

Mineral	Food Source	Needed For
Calcium	milk, eggs	building strong bones and teeth
Iodine	seafood, iodized salt	making a chemical that controls oxidation
Iron	fruits, beans, eggs	building red blood cells
Phosphorus	cheese, meat, cereal	building bones and teeth
Potassium	bananas, potatoes	keeping muscles and nerves healthy
Sodium	meat, milk, salt	keeping muscles and nerves healthy

LIFE SCIENCE GLOSSARY

Adaptation — a change in structure, function, or form that helps an organism adjust to its environment

Amphibians — the class of vertebrates, including frogs, toads, and salamanders, that begins life in the water as tadpoles with gills and later develop lungs

Angiosperms — a class of plants which includes the flowering plants and which is characterized by having seeds enclosed in ovaries

Antennae — a pair of movable, jointed sense organs on the heads of insects and other related organisms that are used for taste, touch and smell.

Arachnids — the class of arthropods, including spiders and scorpions, which have four pairs of legs, no antennae, and which breathe through lung-like sacs or breathing tubes

Arthropoda — the phylum of invertebrate animals with jointed legs and a segmented body such as insects, crustaceans, arachnids, etc.

Benedict's Solution — a blue liquid that is used to test for sugar

Biochemistry — the branch of chemistry that deals with plants and animals and their life processes

Biome — an extensive community of plants and animals whose makeup is determined by coil and climate

Botany — the study of plants

Bulb — an underground plant structure which has roots and which consists of a short stem covered with scales (as in onions and tulips)

Camouflage — body coloring that protects an organism

Carbohydrate — any of certain nutrients made of sugar or starch

Carbon Dioxide — a colorless, odorless gas that is used by green plants and some protists in photosynthesis and which is given off by all living things in respiration

Chlorophyll — the chemical in chloroplasts of plant cells that is needed for photosynthesis

Chloroplast — the chemical in chloroplasm in cells of green plants that contains chlorophyll (photosynthesis takes place in the chloroplasts)

Chordata — the phylum of animals with an internal skeleton

Chromosomes — microscopic, rod-shaped bodies, which carry the genes that convey hereditary characteristics and which are consistent in number for each species

Coelenterata — the phylum of animals with central cavity and tentacles

Commensalism — a relationship in which one organism lives on another without harming it

Crustaceans — the class of arthropods, including lobster, crab, and shrimp, that usually live in the water, breathe through gills, and have a hard outer shell and jointed appendages

DNA — (deoxyribonucleic acid) the acid in chromosomes that carries genetic information

Echinodermata — the phylum of marine animals with a water vascular system and usually a hard, spiny skeleton and radial body (starfish, sea urchins, etc.)

Ecology — the study of the relationship between plants, animals, and their environment

Ecosystem — a system consisting of a community of animals, plants, and bacteria and its interrelated physical and chemical environment

Environment — the part of the biosphere surrounding a particular organism

Fertilization — the joining of nuclei of the male and female reproductive cells

Food Chain — the path of food energy from one organism to another in an ecosystem

Fungi — a kingdom of plant-like organisms that are parasites on living organisms

Science Yellow Pages, Rev. Ed.

or feed upon dead organic material and which lack true roots, chlorophyll, stems, and leaves, and reproduce by means of spores

Gymnosperms — a large class of seed plants which have the ovules borne on open scales (usually in cones) and which lack true vessels in the woody tissue (pines, spruces, cedars, etc.)

Habitat — the type of environment suitable for an organism; native environment

Heredity — the passing on of traits from parents to offspring by means of genes in the chromosomes

Inherited Traits — traits that are passed on from parents to offspring

Larva — the free-living, immature form of any animal that changes structurally when it becomes an adult (the second stage of insect development)

Mammal — a warm-blooded vertebrate that produces milk to feed its young

Minerals — certain elements essential to the proper functioning of living organisms

Mollusca — the phylum of invertebrates characterized by a soft, unsegmented body (often closed in a shell) and which usually has gills and a foot (oysters, snails, clams, etc.)

Molting — a process by which an animal sheds its outer covering

Nocturnal Animal — an animal active mainly at night

Nucleus — the central mass of protoplasm present in most plant and animal cells that contains the hereditary material and controls the life functions of the cell

Nutrient — a chemical substance found in foods which is necessary for the growth or development of an organism

Offspring — a new organism produced by a living thing

Organ — a group of specialized tissues that work together to perform a special function

Organism — a living thing

Parasite — an organism that lives on or in the body of another organism from which it derives sustenance or protection without benefiting the host and often causing harm

Photosynthesis — the process in which green plants use the sun's energy to produce food

Pollen — the yellow, powder-like male reproductive cells formed in the anther of the stamen of a flower

Pollination — the movement of pollen from stamen to upper top of the pistil of a flower

Porifera — phylum of chambered animals (sponges) that live in water

Protein — any of a large class of nitrogeneous substances consisting of a complex union of amino acids and containing carbon, hydrogen, nitrogen, oxygen, often sulfur, and sometimes other elements; proteins are essential for the building and repairing of protoplasm in animals

Protists — Kingdom of simple organisms, mostly one-celled; most do not make own food

Protoplasm — the essential living material of all animal and plant cells

Protozoa — the phylum of mostly microscopic animals made up of a single cell or group of identical cells and living mainly in water (many are parasites)

Reptiles — cold-blooded animals with scales; live mostly on land and breathe air

Sepals — the green leaf-like structures that surround the bottom of flowers

Vertebrates — animals with backbones

Vitamins — organic substances essential for the regulation of the metabolism and normal growth and functioning of the body

Zoology — the study of animals

Zygote — a cell formed by fertilization